COMPETENCY-BASED
COUNSELING

CREATIVE PASTORAL CARE AND COUNSELING SERIES
Howard W. Stone, Editor

BOOKS IN THE SERIES

Crisis Counseling (revised edition)
Howard W. Stone

Integrative Family Therapy
David C. Olsen

Counseling Men
Philip L. Culbertson

Woman-Battering
Carol J. Adams

Counseling Adolescent Girls
Patricia H. Davis

Cross-Cultural Counseling
Aart M. van Beek

Creating a Healthier Church
Ronald W. Richardson

Grief, Transition, and Loss
Wayne E. Oates

When Faith Is Tested
Jeffry R. Zurheide

Competency-Based Counseling
Frank N. Thomas and Jack Cockburn

CREATIVE PASTORAL CARE AND COUNSELING

COMPETENCY-BASED COUNSELING

Building on Client Strengths

Frank N. Thomas and Jack Cockburn

FORTRESS PRESS   MINNEAPOLIS

COMPETENCY-BASED COUNSELING
Building on Client Strengths

Scripture quotations, unless otherwise noted, are from the Revised Standard Version Bible, copyright © 1946, 1952, 1971 by the Division of Christian Education of the National Council of the Churches of Christ. Used by permission.

Map p. 52 adapted from *The New Language of Change: Constructive Collaboration in Psychotherapy,* ed. S. Friedman. Copyright © 1993 Guilford Press. Used by permission.

Excerpt p. 123 copyright © 1996 Reuben Welch. Used by permission.

Cover design: Brad Norr
Cover photograph: Copyright ©1998 PhotoDisc. Used by permission.

Library of Congress Cataloging-in-Publication Data

Thomas, Frank, 1953–
    Competency-based counseling : building on client strengths / Frank Thomas and Jack Cockburn.
       p.   cm. — (Creative pastoral care and counseling)
    Includes bibliographical references (p.   ).
    ISBN 0-8006-2977-9 (alk. paper)
       1. Pastoral Counseling.   I. Cockburn, Jack, 1954– . II. Title. III. Series: Creative pastoral care and counseling series.
    BV4012.2.T48   1998
    253.5—dc21

98-38157
CIP

The paper used in this publication meets the minimum requirements of American National Standards for Information Sciences—Permanence of Paper for Printed Library Materials, ANSI Z329.48.1984.

Manufactured in the U.S.A.   AF 1-2977

02   01   00   99   98   1   2   3   4   5   6   7   8   9   10

ACKNOWLEDGMENTS

From Frank Thomas:

Highest praise must go to my wife, Lori, whose creative suggestions, tireless editing, and loving encouragement took this project from a dream to a reality.

Many have guided me through the years, sharing their wisdom and bringing grace and hope to my journey. I wish to especially acknowledge Steve Brachlow, Tom Chancellor, Michael Durrant, Brad Keeney, Glenn Loy, Tim Murdock, Patrick O'Malley, Larry Powell, Denny Thum, and Kirke Wheeler for friendship and faithfulness.

And for my mother, Marlys, who got me started in my spiritual travels, thanks for persisting.

From Jack Cockburn:

I wish to thank my wife, Elizabeth, and my children, Ashlee and Matthew, for their loving support. A special thanks to Doug Dickens, Professor of Pastoral Ministry, Southwestern Baptist Theological Seminary, for his early influence in championing the notion that ministry takes many shapes. Lastly, to my colleagues and mentors from Texas Woman's University, I am forever in their debt.

From both:
A special thanks:

to Michael Durrant for his trailblazing work in competency based counseling and his valuable efforts to support us in this project; to Howard Stone, who planted the idea of this book and nurtured it in his own special way; to Howard Clinebell, who offered important ideas from the first draft though the publication; and to Henry French and the editors of the Creative Pastoral Counseling and Care series at Fortress Press for their diligence and labors.

95641

CONTENTS

EDITOR'S FOREWORD

It's natural for counseling to focus on problems. People come telling counselors of their problems. We, as counselors, talk with them about those problems. We get details of their difficulties, discover how long they have been occurring, and determine the extent of impairment caused by them. People who seek help frequently find themselves overwhelmed by their problems; they can think of little else. In response to these people, many counseling approaches—and, indeed, most pastoral counseling methods—also focus major energy on the problem. These approaches focus on exploring counselees' liabilities. Frank N. Thomas and Jack Cockburn, in *Competency-Based Counseling,* turn everything upside down. They focus on counselees' strengths. They help counselees recognize their competencies and assist them to use those skills to resolve their dilemmas.

Thomas and Cockburn suggest that the central component of all pastoral counseling is the attitude of pastoral caregivers toward counselees. The authors state that pastors have to believe that counselees, in spite of all their past and present problems, have the resources necessary to make changes needed to address their difficulties. Instead of pastoral caregivers seeing counselees primarily as individuals with problems, they need to view counselees as people who have the necessary competencies to resolve their difficulties. Thomas and Cockburn maintain that counselees have competencies, and they base their pastoral counseling on revealing the gifts and graces of those individuals who seek help.

The reader will notice rather quickly that when competency-based counseling is used, the pastoral caregiver does not focus on the counselees' deficits, but on their strengths and, in so doing, "stand[s] disfunction and pathology on its head." The method of pastoral counseling proposed is not the power of positive thinking. Neither is it Pollyanna. It is realistic. It recognizes that we live in a world of injustice, corruption, and greed. It does not pretend that sin does not exist. Rather it assists individuals to get "unstuck" within the bounds of their own finite freedom in a world where evil does exist. It helps individuals recognize and use their own resources to address the problems that brought them to counseling.

Many parish pastors will find that the method of counseling suggested in *Competency-Based Counseling* is very much like what they are already doing. What Thomas and Cockburn do is refine and detail the method of counseling that many clergy have been doing for years. Nevertheless, pastoral caregivers, who believe that people cannot be helped unless their problems are explored in-depth, will find this book unsettling. On the other hand, clergy, who recognize that individuals in their congregations have gifts and graces that can be used to effectively resolve their problems, will discover in this book a breath of fresh air.

Competency-Based Counseling is a part of a recent trend in pastoral counseling that recognizes most counseling in ministry is brief and the consequent need to develop new methods of care addressing this fact. I found this book beneficial in strengthening the way I already do counseling. The authors, instead of pointing out the problems that I (and other clergy) experience in our counseling, focus and help to build upon the strengths and gifts that most of us in ministry bring to counseling enterprises.

This is a thoughtful, reasoned book by two very experienced pastoral counselors. It is my hope that *Competency-Based Counseling* will challenge you to examine your counseling methods and strengthen your entire pastoral caregiving ministry.

HOWARD W. STONE

FOREWORD

Not another Christian counseling book!

Counseling and self-help books are appearing in a continuing flood and are potentially making every reader an expert in dealing with childhood wounds, codependency, and other newly-discovered forms of pathology. In traveling around various parts of the world, I have seen the books that fill the shelves in airport and hotel bookstores—surely a good test of what people are reading. These titles are all concerned with the toxic effects of childhood experiences or with claiming, reclaiming, or achieving various things that are missing from our lives. One writer said recently, "You don't have to be the son or daughter of an alcoholic to be codependent. Any critical parent will do." The starting point for most of these books seems to be that being wounded, sick, or codependent is always somebody else's responsibility. Whatever my problems are, "any critical parent will do"—it's not *my* fault.

This trend in secular society has been paralleled in Christian literature. When I last visited my local Christian bookstore, there were even more shelves devoted to books that offer similar answers to problems of depression, anxiety, difficult behavior, or problematic relationships for Christians. Most of these books talk about how problems are due to the effects of difficult/critical/pathological parents, or are the result of particular patterns of child-rearing. Many of these books seem to suggest that whatever problems their readers might be facing are somehow due to the trauma of childhood or due to the faults of their parents and require some process of "coming to terms" with these factors. Many books written for parents contain warnings of the damage they might do their children if they are not careful.

Christian literature on counseling and problems has, apparently uncritically, taken on these latest trends in secular psychology. This presents both practical and theoretical/theological difficulties. Practically, approaches that see almost all personal or relationship difficulties in terms of pathology, childhood trauma, or deep unresolved issues present a situation with which the pastor is not trained to deal. If all difficulties require the resolution of deep, pathological disorders, then the pastoral counselor's role is reduced to supporting and referring the client to a more qualified expert. At a theoretical and theological level, the problem relates to the question of personal responsibility.

It is clear that our childhood experiences do have an effect on our development. For example, the Bible talks about original sin—suggesting that we are all destined to sinfulness from birth—and talks of the sins of the father being visited on the sons. What happens in previous generations certainly leaves its effects on us. However, the Bible also says that we are responsible for our behavior. It talks about how God holds us responsible for what we do. Original sin (or genetics) may be an explanation for how our behavior happens but is no excuse when we face the divine standards.

I have always been uncomfortable that some Christians so easily adopt psychological explanations for problems as if these somehow absolve us from personal responsibility.

So, this book from Frank Thomas and Jack Cockburn comes as a welcome relief. Here is a book that gets around the issue of "who is to blame" for the problem (therefore avoiding the question, "Who is not responsible?") and focuses on how to build a solution to whatever the problem is. The competency-based counseling model they present offers a radically different way of thinking about counseling. This approach answers both the difficulties I have suggested above. It offers pastors a practical way of being helpful with whatever problems people present; and it offers a way of helping people take responsibility for their situations and behavior.

In my own practice, I have found that the process of helping a client achieve things that are less depressed, more communicative, or less violent is a process of the client taking responsibility for a more functional, more helpful approach. It has not been necessary to attribute responsibility (or blame) for where the problem came from—it may not even have been necessary to know where the problem came from—rather, it has been important to help clients accept responsibility for the solution, or the desired outcome.

This distinction is profound—what Thomas and Cockburn are about is helping the people with whom they work feel responsible for being successful and competent. As people are able to accept responsibility for their *future* and their present, then the past can recede as they exercise control over where their lives and relationships are headed. Thomas and Cockburn suggest that this approach helps people go out and get on with their lives in a way that is successful.

Of course, if the focus is on how things can be different rather than on what caused these difficulties, then the pastoral counselor is freed from the demands of diagnostic precision and is able to use practical strategies to help his or her clients. Thomas and Cockburn have written a book that considers the assumptions of a counseling approach—how we think about what we do. They invite their readers to entertain some ideas about problems, solutions, counseling, and change that are quite different from the ideas with which many are familiar. Some will find these ideas welcome; others may experience some discomfort at first. The book, however, is not just about theory and assumptions. The authors offer a practical map for the competency-based counselor, with step-by-step instructions and plentiful examples.

Frank Thomas and Jack Cockburn have managed to write a book in a manner that is consistent with what they practice and believe. They present an approach that seeks to be cooperative, to work with clients rather than work on them, and which focuses on what works rather than what is going wrong. They present their approach in a way that seeks to work with their readers, to meet them in their practical situations, and to help them feel more competent in their counseling. While the focus is clearly on what we can do with our clients, the overarching sovereignty of God is also evident.

Read this book once to appreciate how simple the ideas and strategies are. Read it again to appreciate how profound the ideas are.

No, this is not just another Christian counseling book!

MICHAEL DURRANT
Counseling and Family Therapy Program
Psychology Department
University of Western Sydney Macarthur, Australia
Chairman, Australian Fellowship of Evangelical Students

INTRODUCTION

Recently, when I (FNT) was out of town doing research presentations and live demonstrations of competency-based counseling, a counselee I hadn't seen in over a year called and left messages on my voice mail. She sounded concerned but not desperate. Because I was only returning emergency calls, I gave her a call when I returned.

Maggie[1] and I met briefly for five sessions nearly a year ago, but she had previously spent nearly two years with other counselors in another part of the state, and I knew that she placed a high value on counseling. To be honest, when I returned her call I expected to have a conversation about some personal problem Maggie was experiencing. All she wanted, however, was the name of a counselor to pass on to her employer, who lived a great distance from my office and was having some family problems.

As we talked, I asked how things were going for her and she replied that they were "going quite well." She was working part-time as an office manager and enjoying it immensely. Her daughter's troubles with dating and her husband's depression, which had led her to seek counseling with me, were not problematic. She casually mentioned that her daughter had failed the past semester of college. To my delight, Maggie's attitude toward her daughter's grades in college was to "realize I can't change her, so . . . I'll just keep on doing what I know works with us and trust she'll come around!" She also told me her husband wasn't depressed as often as he was in the past, and their marriage was solid and satisfying to her. A year after our brief time together, Maggie continues to be competent in her personal and professional life, much to the amazement of her family.

Prior to our counseling together, Maggie was taking the problems of the entire world upon herself. If her daughter was in trouble at school, Maggie went to the principal and fought for her—even if her daughter was obviously breaking the rules. If her husband had a time of depression, Maggie felt it was her job not only to bring him out of it

1

but also to change herself, believing that if she would simply change enough, she could prevent his depression. In fact, most of the time Maggie spent in counseling prior to our meeting focused on her "codependency" and the problems this brought about in her family. But, after only the few sessions we had together, Maggie was able to turn her life around in a way that continues to endure. Not only is she surviving—she is thriving!

We have to admit, we still hold our collective breath when a former counselee calls! We think most of us do—as much as we try to convince ourselves that counseling works, we are often surprised when it endures. In spite of our trepidation and lack of perfect faith, however, we are convinced that counselees continue to be resourceful long after counseling ends. They prove it to us week after week and year after year in the counseling sessions we hold, and our follow-up calls reveal their continued competence without the aid of counseling.

PASTOR AS PROFESSIONAL HELPER

We talk to pastors and church staff members regularly because we are part of them. Frank is a supervisor and faculty member in both family therapy and pastoral counseling; Jack is a staff counselor and educator at a church as well as a medical family therapist. Our conversations with the men and women "in the trenches" lead us to believe that (1) there are plenty of people who seek their help; and (2) the helpers would like to work themselves out of the "pastoral counselor" job!

Even though the raw numbers have decreased with time, most people still say they would seek out a member of the clergy or a physician for help if faced with a situation requiring professional assistance. Clergy see the most diverse types of problems of any of the helping professions, ranging from adjustment problems to suicide or murder. According to Veroff and his colleagues, people who sought help from a member of the clergy perceived the services they received as helpful 80 percent of the time. This was a higher satisfaction rate than those received by physicians, lawyers, and all other professional mental health service providers. It appears that members of the clergy will continue to be sought out for counsel and that they will continue to be helpful to those seeking their assistance. Therefore, clergy must make a number of choices regarding how they will seek to help.

THE STANCE OF THE HELPER

We are convinced that one of the central components to successful counseling is the attitude the pastor takes toward his or her counselees. What leads us to this conclusion? Well, believe it or not, we enlist the opinions of our counselees! Our research of psychotherapy models has led us to the conclusion that most of what passes for "success" is conceptualized and researched from the professional's point of view. That is, very little time has been spent discovering the counselees' attitudes and experiences in therapy. Because of this, recent research[2] has focused upon counselee viewpoints of counseling. What counselees say about their experience with our model is that *the pastor's belief in them as people* is the most important feature of their success. In the words of one woman, "You believed in me before *I* believed in me!"

We believe that our counselees—whatever their problems, past, or context—have resources upon which we must draw in order to move them beyond this point in time in which they are "stuck."[3] This assumption, which rewards us time and time again, is perhaps the cornerstone upon which we build our approach to meeting people who come to counseling.

WHY THE CHANGE TO "COMPETENCY"?

Insight-oriented models have long been the stock-in-trade of pastoral counseling. To us, insight-oriented approaches in counseling are often characterized by belief in the following:

1. People have fixed psychological/emotional traits and disorders;

2. Catharsis, or release of pent-up emotions, is *the* healing event in psychotherapy;

3. There are underlying psychological causes for "symptoms," and amelioration of these symptoms (or complaints) without resolving these cause(s) will lead to further symptoms and pathology; and,

4. Insight (that is, conscious awareness and understanding) is necessary for lasting change.

We have not found assumptions such as these to be particularly helpful. In fact, we have often found them hindering our counseling relationships and the goals clients wish to pursue. In the coming chapters, we will outline assumptions we bring to the counseling setting that build cooperation, minimize pathologizing and victimizing, and allow counselees to discover other aspects of their experiences that empower them toward change. Please keep in mind that all assumptions—including ours—are simply ideas that guide action and cannot be proven or disproven; they are simply useful or not.

Theories that focus on the resolution of problems through changed behavior and interaction have recently blossomed among the mental health professions. The reason: People in pain and crisis need rapid resolution of their immediate problems, and rapid (and durable) change is possible using brief, problem-focused therapies (Weakland 1990; Zeig and Gilligan 1990). One particular type of counseling, called "competency-based" by Durrant (1993), stands out as a particularly vibrant approach to problem resolution that fits well with many pastors' worldviews and ethics.

Competency-based counseling (CBC) is a brief interactional approach to human dilemmas that focuses on people's resourcefulness rather than their deficits. People have a wealth of resources that they bring to any situation, most of which are neglected or forgotten when problems develop. CBC's main focus is bringing forth resiliency, assets, and successful experiences from the counselee's background and utilizing these resources to bring about positive change. In keeping with this theme, the pastor brings his or her own resources to bear on the counselee's problem as well, and the efforts of this cooperative "team" often bring about marvelous results.

People report amazing abilities to cope, change, and succeed in the face of terrific obstacles. A poll conducted by the Gallup organization and reported by Gurin (1990) tells a startling story. Over one thousand Americans were asked if they had successfully overcome a significant emotional, addiction, health, or lifestyle problem during the 1980s. For those who reported such success, a follow-up question was asked: "How did you do it?" The results were overwhelming: over 90 percent of these persons, who, among other things, had suffered heart attacks, lost spouses or children to death, or suffered profound depression, overcame these problems *without professional assistance*. This book concentrates on this kind of resourcefulness—utilizing the combined strengths of parishioners and pastors, the process of counseling can stand dysfunction and pathology on its head.

We believe church leaders—including pastors, youth directors, and pastoral care specialists—will be drawn to the assumptions and methods of this approach because of its positive focus and its ability to make use of personal, family, spiritual, and community strengths. In particular, you will benefit from this approach because CBC encourages strong, healthy relationships while discouraging dependency on "experts." In this approach, the parishioner is the expert on his or her life and problem, while the pastor is a caring "consultant" who empowers the parishioner in his or her process of change.

This book focuses on several points. First, we propose that the pastor needs to have a competency-based "stance" or counseling position in order to be effective within this model. While some guides to the counseling process stress only theory or intervention, we will diagram a way of thinking that will work in concert with a way of acting in counseling. While these assumptions are not unique to CBC, their inclusion is necessary because of our belief that assumptions guide counseling approaches. Our goal is to outline clearly our basic assumptions for you to examine and ponder, and to accompany these assumptions with counseling and research information to support their usefulness.

Second, we will advance a "map" that will guide the pastor in his or her approach when applying this model. Our assumption is that some maps are more valuable than others depending on the goal of the traveler—topographic maps are useful for the hiker, road maps for the automobile driver, and counseling maps for the practitioner. This CBC map will direct the process in the broadest sense, utilizing the assumptions previously outlined to give therapy a direction that will be beneficial, goal-oriented, and immediately helpful to both the counselee and the pastoral counselor.

Next, we intend to expand upon the basic concepts that constitute the "map" to enable you to develop ideas and move you toward immediate success in the implementation of this model. Areas such as socializing, hypothesizing, goal setting, exceptions, strengths and resources, curiosity, and task development will be addressed in a systematic way, with counseling illustrations that will illuminate the process.

To bring CBC alive for the reader, we will focus on case examples in which we applied CBC, illustrating how we have approached a variety of problems, counselees, and counseling situations.

Finally, we'll examine the application of CBC to other settings and contexts. Employing CBC ideas in the areas of premarital counseling, grief work, shepherding programs, conflict resolution training, board and committee work, marriage enrichment, and family wellness will be discussed to whet the appetite of those desiring other practical applications of this approach. Illustrations will be provided to heighten the creativity of the readers as they begin working from our position.

We hope that this book provides a solid foundation for new ways of viewing and doing counseling for the helper involved with people in need. Although many of the ideas as well as much of the content relate to more formal counseling contexts, we have found the CBC approach to be an exceptionally useful tool for work with youth groups, church meetings, and everyday business and personal relationships. We invite you to examine our assumptions, experiment with our methods, and cogitate on our conclusions . . . if they fit, wear them!

1

WHY "COMPETENCY-BASED" COUNSELING?

Tell me to what you pay attention and I will tell you who you are.
—Ortega y Gassett

In our combined total of more than thirty years of counseling experience, we have practiced a number of counseling models and operated under a host of assumptions concerning human beings, God's ways of relating with us, change, and truth. One thing is certain: *Plus ça change, plus c'est la même chose* (the more things change, the more things remain the same). We are not discovering new worlds as we navigate this chapter; instead, we believe we are creating a defensible story about our journey as helpers. As we move from biblical examples to psychotherapy research, from pastoral dilemmas to a brief history of brief counseling, we will try to examine our ideas critically as we write so that you, the reader, may also scrutinize them with care and caution. First, since we are theologians who value revelatory material, let us examine a few stories that relate to competency-based ideas.

BIBLICAL THEMES AND A COMPETENCY-BASED MODEL[1]

Believing Is Not Necessarily Seeing

A well-known scene from the Old Testament (I Samuel 17) finds a young shepherd fresh from the fields standing amid two armies separated by a giant of a man who is calling out to the other side to send in their best soldier. It is not hard to imagine what might have been going through the minds of those individuals witnessing this stand-off between the giant and the armies of Israel. As the young man emerges from the crowd with apparently nothing but a sling and stones, people could probably be seen rubbing their eyes in disbelief. The general consensus might reflect, as do the recorded observations of both a king and the opposing giant, that the young man was nothing but a mere boy. But, as the story unfolds, the reader soon learns that this "mere boy" succeeds not only in bringing down the giant but in later becoming a king himself.

The point? As a military man of his day, the giant Goliath probably made sense of his world in terms of observable strength and sheer numbers as well as his own massive presence. On the fateful day in question, Goliath felt that the victory would be his based upon what he *believed* he saw before him—a mere boy armed with the simplest of weapons. But David knew different: "The Lord, who saved me from the paw of the lion and from the paw of the bear, will save me from the hand of this Philistine" (1 Sam. 17:37a). For Goliath, this situation was more a nuisance than a "real" problem to be dealt with. David, on the other hand, interpreted this as a clear case involving his faith in the God of Israel enhanced by past successes against previously encountered adversaries.

In our approach to working with people, we assume that people are constantly in the process of making sense of the world around them by drawing distinctions. This process allows people to interpret meanings they assign to events in order that they may be arranged within some meaningful framework. We contend that difficulties generally arise when events and their associated "frames" are made sense of in a particular way that lays the foundation for replication and predominance over time. Cade and O'Hanlon (1993) suggest that having frameworks is not as problematic as forgetting that they are just exactly that and not the "truth" or "reality" (see Watzlawick 1990).

When encountering a problem, people generally employ what they believe will be the best solution for alleviating the situation at hand. As with Goliath's case of mistaken identity, people often confuse what they see with what they *believe* about what they see. In addition, a problem may assume a Goliath-like posture because of what people associate with deep-seated, past-oriented, or causal explanations whose "reality" casts a shadow over past successes, resources, or exceptions. Our approach is always biased towards acknowledging the tremendous potential of people and the inherent flexibility of frameworks.

Doing Something Different

There is a story in Exodus (chapter 18) involving a man and his father-in-law. The man had many responsibilities, among them to be arbiter and teacher of the people. As the man worked diligently from sunup to sundown to resolve the multitude of cases brought before him, his father-in-law was troubled by the fact that others were doing nothing. Suspecting that his son-in-law could not continue doing this indefinitely, the father-in-law expressed his concern. The man replied that the work was his responsibility. The sage father-in-law suggested that while the man was indeed God's representative, he might better fulfill his responsibility by selecting other capable men to handle the simple cases, leaving the man free to handle the more difficult ones.

Jethro's advice to Moses underscores what we mean when we ask people to consider doing something different. When we encounter people working harder at negotiating their difficulties, we often find them doing "more of the same"; that is, they are trying to resolve their problems by applying ideas of what they believe *should* work over and over and over again. We search for a current or hypothetical way, however small, of doing something different from previous attempted solutions—as Watzlawick, Weakland and Fisch (1974) might say, going outside the box. One of our fundamental assumptions revolves around the notion that it is usually the attempted solutions that people employ that maintain the problem. Moses was caught up doing more of the same, which was not working for him. In the search for different solutions, the maxim becomes, "If at first you don't succeed, do something different."

Connected to this notion of difference is Michael White's idea that the person is not the problem—the *problem* is the problem. Jethro did not accuse Moses of egotism or ineptness but rather, conveyed an appreciation of Moses' call in light of specific situational demands made upon his son-in-law. Moreover, Jethro created choice in the context by insisting that Moses still continue to minister but in a very different and, most importantly, more effective manner.

It is somewhat humorous to note that at the end of the story, Moses sends Jethro on his way back home. Like Moses, people engaged with a view toward their competency will have as part of their goal a clear idea about how "we will know when we no longer need to meet like this." Apparently Moses knew.

Changing the Viewing

In the third chapter of I Kings, a wise king was confronted with a seemingly impossible dispute involving a child custody case. Before the king stood two women, each arguing that she was the real mother of the infant. After hearing a heated exchange over the truthfulness of each side of the story, the king requested that a sword be brought in so that the child might be cut in two. The command prompted one woman to relinquish her claim to the child rather than see the child perish. As a result, the king commanded that the child be given to that woman because only the real mother would choose to lose possession of the child in order to save its life.

What did Solomon do? From our perspective, he altered the course of the problem by moving from a frame of "baby as a human being," caught between competing claims, to "baby as object," subject to distribution. We like to think of this as an example of changing the viewing of the problem, what is usually referred to as *reframing*. Briefly stated, reframing can be thought of as offering a new description of a context that makes room for different, yet meaningful, re-viewing (Watzlawick, Weakland, and Fisch 1974). As in the biblical example above, it is important that the reframe fit the context so that the creation of new frames is not imposed externally with no appreciation of the subjective experiences of the parties involved. The frame offered by Solomon simply and effectively moved one woman to view the situation in the context of motherhood and not simply ownership. Reframing, therefore, requires an attentiveness and sensitivity to all aspects of a person's experience. In addition, the success of a reframe is evidenced by its utilization outside the helping encounter where people live.

Defining the Expert

In Mark, chapter 10, there is a simple yet profound story about a much beloved teacher who was on a journey to a famous city when he was accosted by a blind man by the side of the road. Those traveling with the teacher met the man's pleas for help with reprimands and reproaches. The teacher stopped and told the others to bring the blind man to him. As the man approached the teacher, the teacher asked what the man desired of him. Because of the man's faith, he immediately received his sight.

This would not be the only occasion on which Jesus' interactions with people would be prefaced with a question like the one posed to the blind man on the road to Jericho. Although the answer to such questions at times seemed apparent, it was important that Jesus hear the request spoken by the person he addressed. In most cases, the action taken by Jesus was constrained by and limited to the verbal description of need given by the individual. In addition, following each of these interactions Jesus minimized his own role in the healing process by emphasizing the recipient's faith and relationship to God. What is important here is that this process made allowances for the experience of people and their ability to use their faith to bring about positive influences with regard to their relationship with God. This in turn supports the idea that they could maintain the capacity to sustain themselves through their relationship with God both now and in the future.

In our approach to working with people, the observations above support what is thought of as acknowledging the expertise of an individual. Jesus focused on what the man said he wanted rather than imposing his agenda. This idea posits that the experience, belief, and values around a problem are not only respected but supply the frame by which the conversation will be negotiated. In this type of exchange, individuals are free to examine meanings and actions in a frame that does not adhere to the overlaying "map" of another's (the right or the only) experience. It is through curiosity and respect that new landscapes can emerge which allow people to participate and assume greater ownership of their abilities.

Jesus' interactional method with people consistently acknowledged the use of their free will in securing long-term resolutions. He did this by maintaining a gentle and respectful attitude when providing feedback and refraining from using coercive language with those who chose alternative courses of action. The example offered by Jesus of refraining from taking the credit for someone else's success places the ownership and resource squarely in the lap of the recipient.

Lest it go unsaid, we are not advocates of mere listening as an effective way to work with people. Quite the contrary, we think our approach offers an expertise in having certain types of conversations that emphasize the importance of not disempowering people. These biblical stories relate to major themes in competency-based counseling, lending support to its relevance for those of us who value faith. Other avenues offer evidence, including research on the effectiveness of counseling.

"REALITY" OR REALITY?[2]

Whenever we discuss our work, someone invariably comes up with the following question (in some shape or form): "Are you saying that all of reality is just made up?" Instead of beginning a protracted epistemological discussion, we hope you will settle for a few comments. Rather than debate the existence of absolutes (in which we do believe), we hold that social reality is a construction of participation in language. Since we are dealing with people's *perceptions* of their lives and problems, counseling is attempting to change not absolutes but experience. The meanings people ascribe to their experiences are not fixed—they are malleable and constantly subject to new information and interpretation (Gergen 1994). While we accept that there are realities (we would not deny our own existence, for example), we also know that there are enormous variations in the ways people apply their understanding and how they make sense of their lives.

For example: People who apply Jesus' teaching about "denying yourself" in a way that leads to isolation and depression (a common presenting difficulty for pastors) are not just subject to "faulty teaching" or "erroneous understanding"—their perception of this idea and its application to their own lives is affected by other experiences, personality, relationships, and so on. In our pastoral counseling approach we do not seek to excuse wrong by making it relative; instead, we believe we propose new ways for people to take responsibility differently, even from their "stuck" positions.

Therefore, when we speak of reality in this book, please keep in mind what we *are* saying, not what we are *not* saying. This way, we will all be in the same ballpark.

RESEARCH SUPPORTING THE VERITY
OF SHORT-TERM COUNSELING

Some helpers have the luxury of counseling with people for "as long as it takes." A myth has developed in the helping professions that one can and should use his or her training in in-depth psychology, analysis, or other long-term models to help people solve problems, understand their lives, or move beyond their pain. The facts of practice, however, do not line up with this assumption.

The average duration of counseling, whether it be in a private or a community-based setting, is between four and eight sessions. People who come for help do not expect to do continuous counseling for months or years. In one study, 65 percent of counselors preferred to continue the counseling relationship over fifteen sessions, while only 12 percent of counselees expected counseling to take that long (Pekarik and Wierzbicki 1986). Generally, clients expect to remain in counseling for fewer than ten sessions over the course of less than three months. Whatever the theoretical orientation or methods of the helper, counseling is usually short-term.

Other research (Bergin and Garfield 1994; Koss and Shiang 1994; Lambert, Shapiro, and Bergin 1986; McKeel 1996; Smith, Glass, and Miller 1980) supports the idea that doing counseling briefly is both efficient and effective. As stated by Koss and Butcher (1986), "Brief treatment methods have generally the same success rates as longer term treatment programs" (p. 627) (see also Garfield 1994, Koss and Shiang 1994, McKeel 1996). Up to 75 percent of those counselees who report a benefit from counseling receive that gain within the first six months, with 40 percent of counselees terminating after the first or second session. The greatest benefit happens in the first six to eight sessions, followed by continuing but decreasing positive impact for the next ten sessions. Many people seeking help report significant positive change after only one session. Overall, the picture seems to be this: Large numbers of people will terminate counseling before the counselor and the counselee mutually agree upon completion. People normally do not stay in counseling until the counselor feels the process is finished.

Brief counseling in the tradition of the Mental Research Institute (MRI) Brief Therapy Center in Palo Alto, California (Weakland et al. 1974), and the Brief Family Therapy Center in Milwaukee, Wisconsin (de Jong and Hopwood 1996, de Jong and Berg 1998, de Shazer et al. 1986, McKeel 1996), has been well researched over the past forty years. Many critics of brief counseling have stated that short-term, time-limited treatment does not endure; however, results are to the contrary. Self-studies (de Jong and Hopwood 1996, de Shazer 1991), external outcome audits (Koss and Butcher 1986, Koss and Shiang

1994), and independent research (Metcalf and Thomas 1994, Metcalf et al. 1996, Fisher 1980, Fisher 1984) overwhelmingly support brief counseling as an effective approach to problem resolution, with the added benefit that people tend to report a continuation of positive change over time. (For an excellent review of research on short-term and time-limited counseling, see Stone [1994] and Miller, Duncan and Hubble [1997].)

It is also important to acknowledge the place of *counselor training* and *clinical experience* when discussing brief approaches. Some studies suggest that counselors with more counseling experience have greater success in counseling outcomes, while others found no difference in outcome between experienced and inexperienced counselors. Burlingame and his colleagues (1989) discovered that "therapists who received more training in time-limited therapy had clients who displayed greater improvement on several measures of outcome" (p. 311). On the other hand, a recent study by Lyman, Storm, and York (1995) found that, contrary to many long-held beliefs in the counseling field, the counselor's life experience is not a good predictor of success. Perhaps the salient point of this research is that *one should seek supervision and training to become a better competency-based counselor*. We thoroughly endorse peer supervision if professional training is not available, as others who work with the same assumptions, populations, and restrictions may be helpful in one's professional efficiency and effectiveness.

What does this mean? Well, for the young, inexperienced reader, keep in mind that there is hope! Age, diverse life experience, and counseling experience will probably help you be a better counseling pastor, but that doesn't mean you cannot do effective counseling right now.

We will spend a bit more time on brief counseling and researching the results of this approach later in this chapter. For the moment, we believe it is both responsible and accurate to state that *doing effective counseling briefly is a necessity for every human service professional, and this is especially true for pastors who are the front-line service providers in the American culture.*

WHAT KINDS OF PROBLEMS CONFRONT
THE PASTOR "IN THE TRENCHES"?

Of this one thing do I fear. Not to be worthy of my sufferings.

—Tchaikovsky

Below are a few examples of complaints presented during a typical day:

"I'm so anxious and overwhelmed it was all I could do just to get here."

"My wife and I have finally decided to get a divorce."

"I just can't live with this depression anymore and it feels like God has forgotten about me."

"My friends at AL-ANON think that I should just hand my problems over to my higher power."

"I'm not sure my fiancée and I should get married right now because we fight all the time about the dumbest things."

It would not surprise many to learn that these problems were not presented in a marriage and family therapy clinic or psychology center but in an urban church office. The incessant demand for pastoral counseling has, over the years, added another dimension to the many responsibilities of ministers, whether they possess special training or not. As more pastors and church staff come into contact with problems once relegated solely to the domain of certain mental health professions, efficient ways for interacting and dealing with emerging issues will be vital.

Betty D., a recently divorced forty-year-old executive and long-standing church member, presented at the church with her daughter Angela (age fourteen) for truancy, suspected smoking and drug use. After a brief conversation with the pair, it became obvious that Betty and her daughter contributed equally to a gradual "escalating sameness" cycle of blaming and withdrawal that intensified as the session progressed. Betty continually expressed concern that Angela's acting out reflected her unhappiness about the divorce. Angela accused her mother of trying to control her life and not allowing her to express herself. Drawing upon an idea of Brian Cade's (1994), the staff helper in this case asked permission to see Angela initially and then subsequently speak with the mother. In keeping with Cade's notion about working with adolescents, the pastoral counselor made it known that "I will not be handing information from one of you to another; what you ultimately decide to share is your business."

Research over the past few decades supports the fact that many have sought and continue to seek assistance for their difficulties at a church or temple. Gurin, Veroff, and Feld (1960) reported that 42 percent of the people seeking help first went to the clergy. McCann (1962) conducted a study which indicated that over half of the people surveyed would consult the clergy first if they needed emotional assistance. Kulka, Veroff, and Douvan (1979) and Veroff, Kulka, and Dorran (1981) cited that 39 percent of those seeking help went to a member of the clergy. Utilizing data from a NIMH study, Larson et al. (1988) suggested that clergy were as likely as mental health providers to be sought out even for major mental health concerns. Lau and Steele (1990), acknowledging an increase in counseling demand, suggested that a majority of ministers appear assured of being engaged in a certain amount of counseling.

JC: So . . . what would you like to have happen as a result of coming in here?

Angela: I don't know. I know Mom is madder than she's ever been over the school stuff. They're telling her that they are probably going to expel me this time 'cause of what's been happening. If I have to repeat this year she's going to kill me. Besides, we haven't been getting along as it is since she got a divorce.

JC: What stuff's happening that you feel is important for me to know about?

A: Well . . . this makes the third time I got caught walking out of the bathroom with my two friends, and a teacher says that we all smelled like cigarettes. Look . . . I smoke in my room at home with the window open all the time but *I was not smoking* at school! The teacher called me a liar and said she was going to report me and my friends so I went back and got into it with a couple of other girls who were in there smoking, and I almost pulled one girl's nose ring right out.

JC: Whew! What do you suppose kept you from yanking that ring right out of there?

A: Well, my problem is that I get angry inside and it just takes over and all I see is red. But as soon as I grabbed for her and felt the ring in my hand I thought to myself, "This has gone too far," and I just let go of it.

JC: How did you decide that it had gone too far?

A: Uh, that's hard . . . its kind of like somebody trying to take control of you and fighting back . . . or something else . . . I'm not sure. I have a bad temper and most of my friends at school know that, so they stay out of my way. But sometimes I can just tell myself that I'm not going to get into it and so I don't.

JC: So is this a taking-charge problem, an anger problem, or a something-else kind of a problem?

A: I don't know. I'll have to think about that for a while.

JC: That's fine . . . it's a hard question and I wouldn't want you to commit too early without really thinking it through. But by the way . . . I was just wondering, since you mentioned it . . . what is different about the times when you just decide not to let this get the better of you?

A: Well, it doesn't help if I'm in a bad mood. If I'm in a good mood then it's easier to tell myself to just blow it off, that it's really not worth it. But if I'm in bad mood it's harder to do.

JC: Let me see if I am hearing you right. Are you saying that there are times when you manage to take charge even if you are in a bad mood?

A: Uh . . . sure. Sometimes it helps to just get away and tune everybody out, and go somewhere and sit down and maybe draw stuff.

JC: Draw? Like what?

A: All kinds of stuff. When I'm in bad moods I'll draw a red hairy monster with fangs and claws but I can draw other stuff, too, if I want.

JC: Does the bad mood monster always look red and hairy with fangs and claws?

A: Yeah . . . well I dunno . . . that's how it always turns out anyway.

JC: You said you draw other things . . . I'm wondering what kind of other things?

A: I've got a notebook of my drawings I could show you . . . all my friends really like my stuff . . . even my mom likes my stuff. My friends even ask me to draw stuff for them, too. I'm pretty good at it too, especially when I set my mind to it. Lately, I haven't done much though.

JC: You know, I'd love to see your work and, yeah, it sounds like art can be a lot of fun when you decide to set your mind to it.

During competency conversations, we remain consistently curious about a person's sense of *agency*, the power to act. Investigating the times when one overcomes the temptation to give in to a problem and the context involved is vital for any cocreation of space for alternative descriptions of people and their problems. Not only has Angela described exceptions to her "monster," she has a good idea of how to overcome its influence and even what it looks like.

In a survey of Church of Christ pastoral counselors reported by Lowe (1986), the issues as presented by counselees were reported to be (in order of their frequency): marital problems, salvation or spiritual concerns, depression, anxiety, guilt, and parent-child problems. This reflects the findings of Virkler (1979) and Rogers (1985) who reported the same issues that precipitated people to approach secular counselors for assistance. Responding to the notion that individuals seek pastoral help only for religious conflicts, Henderson, Gartner, Greer, and Estadt (1992) reported that pastoral counselors are likely to see the same sort of problems as those presented to conventional social-working professionals.

JC: You know, Angela, I was just thinking about what you said and I've got an idea that I would like to share with you about your art. Would you like to hear it?

A: Yeah . . . OK.

JC: Well, my idea was this . . . and believe me when I tell you I'm a little afraid you're going to find it silly . . . and if it's too silly then please tell me at the end. My idea was that since you have such a good picture of the bad mood monster . . . I was wondering—stop me if this gets ridiculous—if we could go over to the children's Sunday School room and maybe you could paint or draw me a picture of the bad mood monster on one of those large easels with every detail you can remember, and—

A: You're right, this is sounding ridiculous!

JC: OK, but catch this part. Do you usually have your cigarette lighter with you?

A: (*Silence*) Sure.

JC: Great. I thought that maybe once you put the finishing touches on all the details, we could let it dry and come back one day and go behind the building and set the monster on fire.

A: What's that supposed to do?

JC: I don't know . . . but doesn't it sound like fun?
A: You bet it does!

Ritual tasks are an attempt to externalize a complaint in order to offer an opportunity for viewing or thinking about it in a way that avoids the "problem saturated" version of a situation (White and Epston 1990); that is, we believe the experience of a problem often overshadows all other aspects of one's experience. Accessing alternative descriptions of one's life or situation allows for new, nonproblematic story lines to emerge. In addition, within our approach, ritual tasks assist the person in identifying a stance or orientation that imparts a greater sense of personal resourcefulness. Rituals may take any form and are best employed in a context of playfulness and curiosity. We avoid assigning any particular meaning to the ritual, leaving that to the person or persons involved. Rituals are not always the end of an interaction with people but may provide a surprising alternative way for future conversations.

Several days later I met with Angela and her mother (this was Angela's decision) in the parking lot behind the Sunday school building at a time at their convenience. Preparation was made by having a hose available, the picture, and Angela's lighter.

A: Well, here goes nothing. (*Lights the picture*)
B: You know, Angela, I've got to say that that is the scariest picture I have ever seen. It reminds me of those superhero cartoon magazines you buy.
JC: It's that good? I don't read the comics anymore so I'm not an expert.
B: I think that she is good enough to be a commercial artist if she wants.
JC: Really? I hear that is great work if you can get it.
A: Mom helped me submit some of my pictures—
JC: It's (*the fire*) really going now.
A: . . . to see if they're as good as everybody says.

As the picture slowly disintegrated and floated off into small bits of black tissue, Angela wiped her hands briefly and, turning to walk away, looked at me and said, "Well now, that's that, isn't it?" Several weeks later I contacted Betty who indicated that Angela had given up cigarettes and was no longer anything but the talented daughter she knew she had. Sometime later, Angela came by and showed me a small but beautiful portrait she had painted of a woman standing in a field of bluebonnets. Asking her what the meaning of the picture might be, she responded, "It's a hidden treasure."

The problems experienced by pastors in our culture are diverse and challenging, exceeding the imaginations of most who venture into the practice of pastoral care and counseling. We believe that every caregiver should have therapeutic approaches or tools at his or her disposal; however, these approaches to problem resolution should be sharp, well defined, and time tested. For these reasons, we propose that the counseling traditions below will be both useful and supportable for the helper in the trenches, adding to your understanding of human dilemmas and to your repertoire of skills.

COMPETENCY-BASED COUNSELING: A BRIEF HISTORY

What can be done with fewer means is done in vain with many.
—William of Ockham, 14th century

All pleasantries ought to be short—and for that matter, gravities too.
—Voltaire

It would be preposterous to suggest that therapy, in the sense of helping the client achieve symptom relief, enhance well-being, and better functioning, should not be as brief as possible.
—Lazarus and Fay (1990)

When we speak of "brief pastoral counseling," we are not referring to some arbitrary optimal number of fifty-minute hours, nor are we insinuating that "brief" pastoral counseling is somehow superior to other forms of psychotherapy. The brief pastoral counseling we refer to has its roots in a rich tradition of authentic, ethical human service delivery dating back over forty years in psychotherapy and even longer in the church's ministry. We believe that it is important to have an historical context provided so that each reader can gain an appreciation of the breadth of scholarship and the careful counseling development of the brief models we have adopted in this book. After all, anyone can create a counseling model—but careful scholarship maintains it.

The Presence of "Brief" in All Counseling Movements

Lazarus and Fay (1990) grapple with defining "brief counseling." "Does 'brief' refer mainly to temporal truncation, or to a specific methodology, or is it defined by the scope and focus of problems addressed? . . . Are the techniques particularly intensive? Are the goals modest? Is brief (counseling) better or simply more practical, though suboptimal?" (p. 38). They wonder whether there would be any designation of "brief counseling" without the "protracted counseling" of psychoanalysis (in which case we would simply call everything except long-term analysis "briefer," by definition).

The fact is that nearly every therapeutic model, from Freud to the present, has provided case illustrations and study of "briefer" treatment. In fact, attempts to shorten analysis were proposed as early as 1920. And this is not simply due to outside constraints. Koss and Butcher (1986) have stated that "it is now generally recognized that patients, when they enter psychological treatment, do not anticipate that their program of treatment will be prolonged but believe that their problems will require a few sessions at most . . . indeed, patients typically come to psychological treatment seeking specific and focal problem resolution, not for general personality 'overhauls' as assumed in the past" (p. 627).

Whether limited by circumstances, presenting problem, choice, or time limitations, *most* counseling is brief, lasting eight sessions or fewer. While nearly every counseling model in the marketplace has now developed a "briefer" format, those that are typically included in the short list associated with competency-based counseling include MRI (Watzlawick, Weakland, and Fisch 1974), solution-focused and its relatives (de Shazer 1985, O'Hanlon and Weiner-Davis 1989), and narrative therapy (White and Epston 1990). The emphasis here will be on the MRI and solution-focused models, because what unites these approaches is that they "are characterized by a pragmatic stance that is focused on the future rather than the past" (Furman and Ahola 1992b, 41). In addition, "the purpose of (these models) is not to 'understand' the cause of a given problem, but to find fertile ways of thinking about it and practical ideas to deal with it" (Furman and Ahola 1992b, 41–42). Further, these brief models "focus primarily on the observable, on what can be described in a clear and concrete way in terms of things and events . . . It is not that we deny the complexity of human experience.

We believe that the further we move away from the observable or describable nuts and bolts of human interaction, the more we risk becoming caught up in our own metaphors and thus imposing them onto our clients" (pp. 51–52). Although elements from several models can be identified in our approach, our emphasis here will be on the MRI and solution-focused models.

"The 1990s are likely to witness a far greater professional commitment to providing relevant, practical, and short-term therapy to all segments of the community" (Lazarus and Fay 1990, 48). Given this reality, we believe an ethical imperative must be recognized: the ethical counselor must develop flexibility in his or her approach to problems, delivering services that can be effective with little time and counselee contact. Competency-based counseling (CBC), from its roots to the present, offers a map for effective and efficient approaches to the pastoral counselor seeking such an option.

Palo Alto/MRI: The Formalization of Brief Therapy

To understand CBC, one must gain an appreciation for the pioneering work of brief/strategic helpers of the past. Although there is no actual point of conception, the earliest attempt to formalize an approach to problem/solution interaction can be traced to the Mental Research Institute (MRI) in Palo Alto, California. Don Jackson, a psychiatrist who trained with Harry Stack Sullivan, founded MRI in 1958. Several groups and talented individuals contributed to this "confluence of influence."[3] They included the anthropologist and communications researcher Gregory Bateson, the pioneering psychiatrist Milton Erickson, communications expert Jay Haley, and chemical engineer John Weakland. At its inception, the MRI's focus was on communication in families and other groups and it evolved from the Palo Alto Project of Bateson, Weakland, Haley, and William Fry, Jr., which lasted from 1952 to 1962. Others who joined the MRI in the late 1950s and early 1960s and who contributed greatly to its theoretical roots include Virginia Satir, Arthur Bodin, Lynn Hoffman, Jules Riskin, and Paul Watzlawick.

Richard Fisch, M.D., started the Brief Therapy Project within MRI. In the spring of 1967, the Project began with three goals: "(1) to find a quick and efficient means for resolving complaints that clients bring to psychotherapists and therapists; (2) to transform therapy from an art into a craft that could be more easily taught to others; and (3) to study change in human systems" (Segal 1991, 171). As one can see, the MRI "brief" approach is not grounded in any particular psychotherapy or family systems counseling approach; instead, it was intended to be utilitarian, interactional, and problem focused, starting with the most specific level of complaint and interaction and working outward. "[The Brief Therapy Center's] original intention was to explore what could be achieved therapeutically in a brief time with a variety of specific problems. The duration of treatment was limited to ten sessions, with very active intervention and a primary focus on the main presenting problem. It was soon found that this approach was effective and that successful resolution of the presenting problem often led to changes in other problem areas as well" (Bodin 1981, 269). The interest of the BTC was in being as close as possible to the behaviors and interactions that maintained what had developed into a counselee's problem. To accomplish this focus, a purposeful emphasis on "what" and "how" was established, and the question of "why" was avoided. This avoidance of "why" was an attempt to move away from the dependence on abstract constructs or attempting to identify intrapersonal states such as "intention," "drive," or "motive" (see D'Andrade 1986), which had dominated psychological theory and practice since its inception.

The MRI approach to problem resolution has spawned a diverse set of counseling and research ventures through the past thirty years. Included in this eclectic list are the Emergency Treatment Project (a twenty-four-hour crisis intervention service center, focusing on victims of assault), Soteria House (an alternative, cost-effective community residential treatment center featuring a no-medication approach for some types of schizophrenia), the Non-labeled Family Project (a longitudinal research project studying nonclinical families), and other unique endeavors. The great variety of research projects and the rich history that continues today is described well by Ray and Weakland (1995) and Bodin (1981). We believe it is sufficient to say that the impact of the Mental Research Institute, and specifically the influence of the Brief Therapy Project, has been pervasive in human service delivery over the past three decades and will continue to exert its influence through such clinicians and scholars as Richard Fisch, Paul Watzlawick, Brian Cade, Wendel Ray, and others.

Enter de Shazer and Solution-Focused Brief Therapy (SFBT)

Steve de Shazer, a social worker and researcher, spent a great deal of time at MRI in the 1970s. He was actively writing during this decade on brief therapies, focusing on strategic approaches to problems (de Shazer 1975, de Shazer 1978). During this same time, de Shazer embarked on a somewhat different path, culminating with the establishment of the Brief Family Therapy Center (BFTC) in Milwaukee and his publications of *Keys to Solution in Brief Therapy* (1985) and the now classic article "Brief Therapy: Focused Solution Development" (de Shazer et al. 1986). Rather than creating a competing model, de Shazer and his associates developed an approach to problem resolution that was purposefully associated with the MRI tradition. De Shazer's emphasis on brevity continued the MRI tradition of "as few (sessions) as possible" (de Shazer et al. 1986, 207), but the central focus of this hybrid approach was the resolution of human problems, *not* brevity. The central difference between the MRI model and de Shazer's approach is found in de Shazer's emphasis on "solutions and how they work" (de Shazer et al., 1986, p. 208). From its inception, this model emphasized several foundational ideas, most of which were congruent with the MRI approach. First, SFBT recognized the importance of context through (1) the importance it attached to human interaction, and (2) its emphasis on the "fit" between the counselee's experience of the problem and the proposed solutions. Second, "resistance" became an interactional dilemma to solve rather than a counselee state. Third, the meaning of a "problem" was dependent on the person making the observation. Fourth, only a small change was necessary to create system-wide changes. And fifth, knowing when a problem is solved was more important than knowing the cause or explanation of the problem. In his seminal paper (de Shazer et al. 1986) de Shazer clearly distinguishes his approach, which came to be known as "solution-focused," from the MRI model and other brief approaches. Some of the central assumptions defining SFBT are:

1. People coming for counseling have complaints, not problems. Therefore, the problem is not a "symptom" of an underlying systemic dysfunction (*à la* Haley and other strategic therapists);

2. The important focus is on the future without the problem, which leads the counselor and counselee(s) to center on current *exceptions* to

the problem and *specific goals* that are directly related to the resolution of the complaint;

3. Solutions may or may *not* follow logically from the presenting problems. Looking in counter-intuitive directions for change may be necessary, as what is *useful* is more important than what is "right"; and,

4. "Creating expectations of change" is paramount in the model, because "what you expect to happen influences what you do" (de Shazer et al. 1986, 213).

De Shazer's influence at BFTC has become greater with time. Among those who have worked with him and gone on to develop hybrids of the SFBT model are Insoo Kim Berg (Berg 1991, Berg 1994, Berg and Miller 1992), Michele Weiner-Davis (O'Hanlon and Weiner-Davis 1989, Weiner-Davis 1992, Weiner-Davis 1995), John Walter (Walter and Peller 1992), and Scott Miller (Berg and Miller 1992; Miller, Hubble, and Duncan 1996), all of whom have written prolifically in both professional and popular circles. The influence of MRI and the solution-focused approaches continues in our work, and we are honored to associate ourselves with this fine counseling tradition that engenders hope, resolves serious human problems, and restores family harmony.

Stories, research, and history: we believe this is the foundation for our work. It is more than personal experience, and its use is defendable. Moreover, placing oneself in a historical tradition provides not only a backdrop for action but also a community for criticism. As we move on to theoretical and counseling assumptions, keep in mind that we draw from a deep well of tradition and research. We are spokespersons, not magicians.

2

ASSUMING A COMPETENCY-
BASED STANCE

We believe that one's assumptions determine one's counseling approach. Most who read this book can recall experiences of heightened anxiety around unexamined assumptions related to faith and the Bible. Do you recall the first time someone pointed out the "footnotes" in your Greek New Testament? Knowing that some texts had little support for accuracy and few manuscripts from which to draw caused both of us to quiver for weeks! To rethink one's basis for faith can be threatening; on the other hand, careful inspection of one's assumptions can lead to refinement and liberation.

When considering a competency-based approach to counseling, one should examine the premises upon which this model is built. If most of these "fit" for you, then application to your particular setting will involve deliberateness and practice. On the other hand, if some of these presuppositions clash with your personal beliefs, then the road to solution orientation may be troublesome. We hold to a simple premise: if you don't carefully examine your assumptions about change, counseling, and people, you are likely to repeat old patterns and fail to apply these new tools and ideas.

There is no "right" way to view things; in fact, there may be many ways to make sense of life that fit the facts equally well. Because of this initial premise, we believe that social reality is something people create together. Below we present and elucidate six theoretical assumptions on which counseling may be based.

1. *Complaints consist of behaviors resulting from the counselee's perception and interpretation of the world* (de Shazer 1985).
   One of the underlying premises of a competency approach is that people are constantly making sense of their lives and their world around them (see von Glasersfeld 1984, Durrant and Kowalski 1993).

27

As a result, what we are dealing with when encountering people's complaints are their perceptions and experiences of their circumstances and not the "truth" or "reality." Indeed, there is no "right" way to view difficulties; in fact, there may be many ways to make sense of life that fit the facts equally well. This underscores the idea that such realities are by and large socially constructed and not created in isolation. Furman and Ahola (1992a) express this idea by suggesting that everybody is influencing everybody. The following case example illustrates how counselees are given the opportunity to evaluate their present circumstances and the influence of others in that process.

Laura, age thirty-three, was referred by a local pastor because of her professed aversion to her newborn daughter. She was seen by one of the authors (JC) for a total of three sessions. The following is an excerpt from the first session and begins with Laura expressing concern over her lack of attention to her daughter Amy, age four months.

JC: So, what brings you here?

L: Well, my pastor thought it would be good to get a second opinion about why Amy and I can't seem to get it together.

JC: What does that mean for you?

L: Well, I prayed and prayed about this baby because we haven't been able to have a child. But ever since she was born I have been tired, I mean so tired that I can't even get the housework done the way I used to. Then Amy cries and wants to be held and it's all I can do just to get her fed and quiet. It wouldn't be so bad but my body feels terrible all day and I didn't know why. My mother was confused about all this because she had four of us and she told me that it was normal to be up and working the next day. My husband finally convinced me to go back to the doctor and to find out what was wrong with me. It didn't take him very long to figure it out either. He told me that I had postpartum depression. When I left his office I felt like God tricked me into having this baby.

JC: I see. That sounds pretty serious. I was just wondering how much of what's been happening is normal for some folks. I mean, could it possibly be God's way of letting you know that it's time to relax and enjoy your baby?

L: (*Smiles*) Well, I don't know about that!

JC: Neither do I.

L: But you know . . . now that you mention it, I have been through an awful lot. Part of my problem is that we live in the country and I don't have any other friends that are pregnant so I don't know what's normal for me yet.

JC: Yeah, I hear being a first-time mom is tough work. I was just wondering: is this a situation where a person could use a little practice?

L: Yeah . . . hey, they say practice makes perfect, don't they?

Furman and Ahola (1992b) suggest that "whenever people communicate in any way, they automatically, overtly or covertly, willingly or unwillingly, influence others to view things the way they view things." In the above case, Laura's perception of the problem had been influenced by not only herself, her mother, husband, and physician but by the lack of peers around her that might have supported more useful or alternative views around competency.

As seen above, making sense of one's world involves negotiations with others in a specific context. For example, when discussing her concerns with her physician, Laura was offered a way to make sense of her condition by a clinical appraisal. With her family, the process was couched in a language of "what could be the matter" or "finding out." Furman and Ahola (1992b) suggest that "whenever a word is used, a chain of associations is triggered and that chain of associations then influences the way a person thinks about things."

To help clarify this last notion, let's consider how Laura's struggle with motherhood and her initial diagnosis might have provoked her imagination. You'll perhaps recall that her presenting comments regarding her condition reflected the use of the psychiatric term "postpartum depression." Even without an intimate knowledge of this terminology, it is not difficult to imagine a train of word associations which could be evoked by such a term. Using this term drew Laura to potentially appraise herself as abnormal, dysfunctional, or somehow deficient in the area of motherhood. More than likely, Laura had not associated early motherhood with a disheartening lack of energy and a pessimistic outlook.

We contend that language influences how people respond to and think about life's difficulties. The selection of a particular term or phrase always leads to a multitude of associations. As Furman and Ahola (1994) aptly point out, "Words used in . . . psychology . . . often tell us little, sometimes almost nothing, about the actual problem, but a great deal about what we should think about it" (p. 58).

On a more humorous note, we would like to share a story we heard concerning motherhood: A recent graduate from a seminary program in the field of marriage and family counseling was called to join the staff of a burgeoning urban church. Among her initial duties as a ministry team member was the implementation of programs which would effectively reach single and new mothers. Bringing her expertise to bear, she instituted her first seminar, titled "The Ten Commandments for Motherhood in Modern Times." Mothers from far and wide came to draw upon her expertise in the hopes of expanding their abilities. She felt that being single with no children presented little if any problem due, in part, to her extensive study of developmental life cycles and contemporary women's issues. She then met the man of her dreams, and sometime later they married and had a baby girl. She then titled the class "Ten Thoughts for Motherhood." A year later the couple found themselves the proud parents of a baby boy. She then named the class, "Ten Tentative Hints for Motherhood." Shortly thereafter they were blessed with another baby girl. After her third child was born, she stopped teaching the class altogether and began support and ministry groups for mothers.

2. Problems are best viewed in terms of interactional patterns that are inadvertently maintained in the hopes of resolving the original difficulty.
Watzlawick and his colleagues (1974) draw a distinction between difficulties and problems and cite three ways people mishandle problems. The first mishandling requires an active response looked upon as necessary but not taken (that is, the refusal to relate to the problem as a genuine problem). The second way of mishandling occurs when particular attempts are taken and they should not be (that is, problems are thought of as either unchangeable or nonexistent). Finally, the third mishandling of problems may assume the form of "mixed messages." This was illustrated by a recent visitor in the church office who presented for marital counseling, indicating that she "wanted her husband to want to want to love her more." (Yes, you read that correctly!)

Common to these observations is the underlying emphasis on explanation or causation. This is usually presented in the form of the question "Why does it happen?" However, as postulated by Gregory

Bateson (1979), an explanation never adds anything to description. In a competency-based approach, it is thought more useful to ask a question such as "What is happening?" than "Why is it happening?" Keeping the emphasis on description (what happened to whom, when, where, and how) leads one *away* from unattainable, poorly-shaped goals and ineffective means and *toward* effective counseling based on achievable ends. This emphasis on description does not negate the possible existence of a cause ("why") or knowing it—we just don't pursue it. Instead, we focus on description because it supplies the data we find more useful in this approach. In CBC, we are interested in pragmatics and utility more than the reasons and explanations "behind" experiences, because we have found this to be a powerful avenue for change.

Another component common to the three ways problems are mishandled are the attempted solutions sought by the three positions. Watzlawick and his colleagues (1974) suggest that many problems escalate if no solution or a wrong solution is attempted—especially if *more* of a wrong solution is applied. This results in what might be called "vicious cycles" that serve to reinforce a "problem-focused" view of the person and other persons involved. Moreover, this is usually accompanied by the assessment of blame which results in the person being seen as the problem as opposed to the problem simply being the problem. Conversely, competency-based approaches embrace the adage that "if it doesn't work, don't do it again. Do something different" (de Shazer 1990).

Our experience has been that individuals presenting for assistance generally persist in holding to an interpretation of either/or outlooks when struggling with problems. That is to say, what they have attempted in the past has, for them, been the logical and correct series of choices. Alternative options outside of those choices are usually regarded as not within the realm of possibility or reason. Often counselees adhere to the attempts at solving problems based on the belief that what they are doing is the *only* avenue for success. It is because of this belief that counselees behave as if the only thing to do is more of the same. This typically results in further attempts, subsequent failures, and possible additional problems.

In words attributed to Gregory Bateson, these attempts might be thought of as an individual's "reality being a matter of faith."

3. *Change is inevitable. If one part of a system changes, other changes will occur. "Change is so much part of living that [people] cannot prevent themselves from changing"* (Berg and Miller 1992, 11).

Our experience has been that counselees typically view the problems they bring to counseling as constant in nature. Often the thought exists that the problem never varies in frequency or intensity. Moreover, if something about the problem does change, it is often constructed as insignificant. We, on the other hand, hold to the assumption that change is constantly occurring, stability is an illusion, and change cannot be prevented. We contend that this pervasive view about the consistency of problems can be developed from two commonly held beliefs.

The first belief is grounded in the statement of "I am (fill in the blank)." It is one thing to say "I am naturally blond" or "I am Italian." These are characteristics that are not subject to alteration because there are not times when one is not (naturally!) blond or Italian. However, we assert that it is something quite a bit different to say that "I am depressed" or "I am codependent." This type of language acts to label individuals and, in so doing, creates the illusion that counselees are mere duplicates of others or that they serve as an example of some category of pathology. This robs both the counselee and the pastor of the uniqueness of each individual's personhood and greatly restricts future interactions. In addition, there is the not-so-subtle suggestion that by labeling someone with a particular problem we possess an understanding of the problem. We follow the lead of Walter and Peller (1992), when encountering the use of "I am so and so" and choose verbs like "says," "seem," "acting as if," or "show." This has the effect of expanding and moving the dialogue to less restrictive possibilities, imparting a respect for the counselee's view, and hinting that other behaviors might be available in other contexts. For example, if someone states that he or she is depressed, our response generally takes the following tack: "So, you say you've been acting as if you're down in the dumps," or, "Well, if I have heard you right, you've been experiencing discontent lately." Substituting active verbs and avoiding "to be" verb forms subtly invites the client away from stagnant to more open, flexible positions, implying that the current state of affairs is temporary and subject to future alteration.

A second commonly held belief involves the tendency for people to seek explanations. Most explanations are born out of the inclination for people to pose the question "Why?" As an example, if an individual is labeled as codependent, then the bias will be to act and speak in ways that offer explanations for codependency. In other words, the "Why?" of the complaint is explained by reference to those origins and behaviors regarded as codependent. We agree with Furman and Ahola (1992b) when they state that "expressions that deal with cause and effect, such as 'because,' 'the reason for,' and 'due to,' are to be abandoned" (p. 13). A competency-based approach spends very little time exploring the so-called inevitable links between a problem and its history. We are far more concerned with a present sense of "What happens?" rather than a past's sense of "Why does it happen?"

Challenging these two beliefs provides space for ideas that suggest that change is so much a part of living that counselees cannot prevent themselves from changing. A competency approach cultivates these ideas about change based upon the counselee's view of the world without the complaint or when the complaint does not occur. By not focusing on problem talk, counselees generally appear more optimistic as together we amplify the talk about exceptions to the problem, entertain "instead ofs," or ask about when things are just a little bit better. As counselees are sent out to examine their lives in light of these discussions, their attention is invited to focus on those actions and experiences which are more competent or in control. Once they have described what pieces or parts were useful in gaining a sense of competency, we like to send them back out with the admonition to "keep it up!"

In our experience, once small changes begin they invariably lead to further changes. This "small change" attitude encourages counselees toward competency and makes even so-called big problems manageable. We agree with Furman and Ahola (1992b) when they insist that: "There are only two ways to help people solve their problems. One is to suggest a new way of *doing* something about it, and the other is to suggest a new way of *thinking* about it (emphasis is theirs). Ultimately even these two choices melt into one" (pp. 17–18).

4. *Rapid change is possible, if not probable.*

I (FNT) had a sixty-seven-year-old woman come to see me upon the urging of her niece, who was a school counselor in the area. Elaine was recently widowed after a long, happy marriage. She lived alone, and she had enjoyed an active social and personal life prior to recent sleeplessness. She stated that she was losing sleep to the point of near exhaustion. Her understanding of the situation revolved around her fear that her only daughter, who had recently had open-heart surgery, might die at any moment. Although her daughter's recovery was constant and hopeful, and in spite of the fact that her daughter had a competent husband and adolescent daughter, Elaine was afraid that she would not be available for her daughter in the event of an emergency. This led to sleeplessness, anxiety, tearfulness, and indecision, to the point that she "was not having her own life."

During our initial session, I was tempted to follow other ideas that might have been helpful—grief and loss models, family structural models, and others passed through my head. However, holding to the "change is inevitable" premise, I began to discover that her situation was *not* constant; that is, there were times she was able to control her tearfulness and indecision, but she had not been paying attention to these. Examining these times of difference and what she did to bring them about, Elaine concluded that she was not helpless and decided to explore other times when the problem was not getting the best of her during the coming weeks.

Our next appointment was her last! Shortly after our initial visit, she noticed that she was less anxious and indecisive when she talked openly with her daughter about her fears and when she was more assertive with her other children and grandchildren. During this two-week period, she discovered that she could take pleasure in allowing others to do things for *her*, which was very different from her servant-like existence prior to that time.

Prevailing understandings in our culture might have placed labels on Elaine such as "codependent"; however, we instead focused on exceptions to her problem that existed side-by-side with her problems, and she was able to access these in a very short period of time. In fact, she told me that she only returned to our final visit to fill me in and let me know that she was fine! A year later, she has maintained her change and continues to control her own life.

5. *Motivation is more likely when people are viewed as competent.*

In the movement toward competency, we feel it is vital from the very beginning to convey to the counselees that their experiences are being heard and validated. This does not stem from the belief that a "baring of the soul" in and of itself is tantamount to change. Rather, this interaction involves attending to the actual language of the counselee and utilizing it in one's own verbalizations. In addition, this forms the basis of future interventions based upon the counselee's worldview, language, and experience. Moreover, interaction around a confirmation of experience allows the counselee to assume a posture that begins to reflect an expertise or competency when relating personal problems. This enterprise is related to a future activity of treatment because we assume that our counselees are also experts in their own future goals. It is our experience that once the "counselee as expert" of their own experience has been offered, people are more easily invited and motivated to develop a sense of control and direction over the therapeutic process and outcome.

The following is an excerpt from the second interview with Laura about her ability as a mother.

L: It helped last week to know that a lot of what I am going through might be pretty much normal for new moms, but I still get depressed about my ability to get things done.

JC: How tough is it to get things done?

L: Well, sometimes it is next to impossible to do even the simplest things around the house. It's like everything takes a special effort.

JC: How do you decide when to use your special effort?

L: I just kind of decide to get with it, you know?

JC: So are there some times when it's hard but you get with it anyway?

L: Sure I wish it was easier with Amy but as my mother says, once you're on this train there is no getting off.

JC: Is there light at the end of the tunnel?

L: Yeah . . . because I still like to have a clean house and it makes me feel better when it finally gets done. It makes me feel like I can handle this responsibility God has given me.

JC: It sounds as though your special effort helps you to be capable of doing a lot more than you give yourself credit for. I wonder what the difference might be if you could call on this special effort more often?

L: I think I would have a lot more good days than bad.

JC: Really! I wonder what might be different if you were to start experiencing more good days instead of bad days?

It is important that we match the counselee's assumptions and basic point of view to our counselee's experience. When using the counselee's language, resources emerge that offer opportunities for alternative descriptions of experience. As the dialogue develops, "a focus upon competences is more likely to lead to our clients noticing and experiencing (their existing examples of) competence" (Durrant and Kowalski 1993).

6. *The relationship between a problem and its solution (s) is not necessarily logical. Complex problems do not necessitate complex solutions. Once you move away from a belief in simple cause and effect, a whole new world of possibilities is open to you.*

Many pastoral counselors believe that problems follow a fixed course—they are born, live a long life, and die independently of the people involved. This way of thinking is widespread in Western culture; in fact, it is so prevalent that most of us see it as true rather than as a viewpoint or explanation. The idea of a "fixed course" of an "emotional injury" is adopting a Western medical analogy that we do not believe. Behavior, emotion, and relationship difficulties do not behave the same way as bacteria, blood vessels, and cancer. Most people hold firmly to the belief that if a person suffers an "emotional injury" in life, it will affect him or her in certain prescribed ways in the future. For example, most people believe that a person who is physically abused as a child is doomed to certain experiences, behaviors, and problems throughout the course of life. Although this way of viewing life is a powerful explanatory tool, it is not very predictive. That is, looking *back* in life from a problem, it is easy to believe that certain events *caused* the current problem (explanation); however, there is little evidence that having an event in one's life will inevitably lead to certain problems (Durrant and Kowalski 1990, Thomas 1995b).

Once a pastor moves away from simple cause-and-effect, he or she also opens up new vistas for change. Working with a future orientation and refusing to allow such limited thinking to dictate the course and duration of change opens up wonderful possibilities for rapid, lasting change.

A newly divorced minister came to me (FNT) for "divorce adjustment therapy." His initial prognosis for his own recovery was poor—he was racked with emotions he did not understand; he felt like a failure in life; he could not concentrate on his work, to the point where he felt he might have to take a month or more of professional leave to "get a grip on this." During our initial interview, I discovered he had mapped out a "course" for his divorce experience from some books he had read. The next description will come as no surprise—he was not doing it correctly, especially the part about "crying to get it out." He fully expected his experiences to follow the course that "divorce adjustment" takes—and he was failing at it!

I began to explore other parts of his experience since his divorce—the facts that were also present but ignored. He had developed some meaningful relationships with other men that he felt had moved him toward recovery; he decided that writing a letter to his ex-wife to say all the things he wanted to say, but not mailing it, would be helpful; and he was able to identify many moments in his life when he was not depressed or angry, including times when he was ministering to others. Equipped with these exceptions, he decided that he "had it on the run" and might not have to go through all the "stages of grief" that had been prescribed by the experts[1] (see Butler and Powers 1996).

We met three times over a two month period, and he left counseling after deciding he had "worked through his divorce" and felt competent to continue on his own. What began as an intractable, insoluble problem requiring lengthy, complex interventions was simply and quickly addressed. This was supported throughout by the belief that it *could* be addressed simply, and that how he solved this problem would not necessarily be logically tied to the "cause" of his problem.

Now, we cannot prove that any of these positions are true—we simply choose to act as though they are because it enhances our pastoral counseling, creates a context of cooperation with counselees, and allows for optimal change within the competency-based approach. We also recognize that ideas have limits—we may have created the "head" in this chapter, but we have no "feet" unless we create clear interpersonal approaches. As Bradford Keeney (1983) has stated, pure theory without pragmatic action is free-associative nonsense (or, faith without works is dead!); however, action without thought is decontextualized and therefore dangerous. Thus, the next chapter focuses on travel—feet, footwear, and maps!

3

A MAP FOR COMPETENCY-BASED COUNSELING
Part I: Getting Oriented

*The map is de-scriptive rather than pre-scriptive. It is not a map
of the "right way" or the "only way" or even the "best way."
Simply, a map is not the territory.*
—Steve de Shazer, *Clues*, 1988, pp. 88, 104

*People are generally better persuaded by the reasons which they have
themselves discovered than by those which have come into the minds of others.*
—Pascal

THE NECESSITY OF MAPS

Let's say you wanted to get from Tucumcari to Cucamonga, a city
about one hundred miles away. Assuming you are unfamiliar with the
Tucumcari area, how would you make the trip? Most of us would say,
"Well, all I need is a road map and I could make the trip with ease." In
an age of nearly unlimited personal transportation options, traveling
in our own automobile seems the simplest and most logical means of
travel. So, it makes sense that you might think of this as the first
option.

Traveling by car may not be the best travel choice, however. Let's
assume, for a moment, that you have many transportation modes at
your disposal. You are not only an Indy-class driver now; you are also
an accomplished kayaker, a world-class hiker, and a qualified helicopter
pilot! If a mountain range were between Tucumcari and your destination, you might wish to fly there in a helicopter. For this trip, a road
map might not be as helpful; instead, an aviation map might be more
useful. If you were going to spend a week hiking to this destination, a
road map would be of no use. Your best choice might be a U.S. Geo-

logical Survey topographical map, or a U.S. Department of the Interior National Forest map that would allow you to locate all of the established trails, logging roads, and unpaved roads between Tucumcari and your destination. Finally, if a navigable river ran from Tucumcari to Cucamonga, you might choose the local 1:10,000-scale topographical map so that you could locate the public and private lands along the way for camping, portage, and rest.

Which map is the "correct" map? Well, none of them is "correct." Depending on the means of transportation, however, one map might be more *useful* to you for your journey. No matter how accurate, detailed, or colorful, no map is the territory—every map is but a representation of a certain aspect of the territory you wish to explore.

A great deal of confusion may arise at this point for you. When moving into the counseling arena, many helpers assume that the map they possess *is* the territory. They presuppose that there is a "correct" way to deal with problems, symptoms, and dysfunction, and that any approach is inadequate (or, worse, will only work on the "surface" but will fail to resolve the "core" cause of this problem). If you are confused at this point, or if you have serious disagreements with these ideas, we ask you simply to read on and pretend for a while that we also have a map, one that may differ from your own but may actually be *more* useful to you as you attempt to help those coming to you for counsel. Although many models of counseling purport to be true, to us they are merely guides that attend to part of people's experiences. When these guides become less useful, or when they do not attend to what needs to be considered, then we believe they can be discarded and replaced with more helpful maps that guide us from Tucumcari to Cucamonga—or, in this case, from problem to solution.

ASSUMPTIONS OF COMPETENCY-BASED COUNSELING: GETTING ORIENTED

Following the theoretical assumptions in chapter 1, here we examine how to pick our course, our mode of transportation, and our destination as we set out on our counseling "journey." If theoretical assumptions guide how one thinks, then counseling assumptions should be viewed as guides to what one does. Every pastoral counselor makes decisions according to some (usually unexamined) set of ideas regarding what is "the right thing to do in this situation." Some are obvious and nearly universal. For example, if a counselee begins to tear up or openly cry, most pastoral counselors attend to the current experience in some way. We know that giving head nods and little "um-hmms"s encourage most people to continue speaking. Most of us also act on the belief that, when in doubt, it is better to do nothing than to do the wrong thing! Although these seem like common sense, they are actually assumptions—uncritically applied presuppositions—upon which we act in the counseling setting.

The competency-based counseling approaches have several guides that give the pastor direction when face to face with the counselee. Learning these guides so that they become second nature will enable the competency-based counselor to make decisions that will give the parishioner's resources the best chance of surfacing and create a context for rapid change.

Dr. Richard Fisch, Director of the Brief Therapy Center at the Mental Research Institute in Palo Alto, California, states his belief that nearly all "therapy" prior to the past century was "brief"; that is, whether the helper was a shaman, a priest, an oracle, a minister, or a mesmerist, the emphasis was on *doing* rather than insight. Both the helper and the person seeking help worked together on a common goal of overcoming some problem or obstacle, stressing *action* for both parties and assuming that change would come about because of the actions taken. He has suggested four elements found in all modern brief therapies (Fisch 1994). These are a good starting point when looking for ways to orient on the trail.

First, the helper must *narrow the "database."* The time spent in counseling needs to focus on the present and possible futures rather than on the past. Such a move does not negate the importance of the past; instead, it simply relegates the past memories of the counselee to a less central position in the counseling activity. The focus of our counseling must be on the present experience of a problem and the future experience of success.

Walter, a man in his mid-fifties wearing a back brace, came to see me (JC) at the church because of depression that, according to him, had been the focus of various treatments for the past three years. He called and made an appointment because "I only think about dying all the time these days." The initial aspect of this interview is offered below.

JC: Since our time together will be short and we cannot get into all that has happened, what do you think is the most important thing for me to know as we begin?

W: Well . . . I lost my job at the airlines several years ago because of a back injury and since then things have gone downhill. It's not like every day is a black cloud, but it seems like things are getting worse. But after I lost my job it seems like what little confidence I had has flown the coop. Besides, I have never had much self-esteem anyway. My wife . . . well, she thinks that it's the medication I've been taking but I won't know for sure until I go back to the doctor. What scares me the most is that the stuff runs in my family.

JC: How might you describe the effect—say, for example, let's take today—that this problem has in your life?

(A preference for allowing the counselee to begin to define the problem—among many possible options—is offered here to acknowledge what he or she has said while seeking additional descriptions more firmly embedded in present experience.)

W: It's as I said over the phone. It's getting so that all I am thinking about is death and dying . . . like, how things would be better if I just up and checked out.

JC: What does this keep you from doing . . . say, like today?

W: Heck, today I could barely get out of bed. I usually stay in bed most of the day, but today I got out. But to answer your question, I usually feel like I can't cope with anything, you know . . . just pull the covers over your head. I'll tell you something else: talking about it seems to make it worse.

JC: Oh . . . so, what might be the first sign that things are getting a little better?

W: *(Pause)* I guess the fact that we are sitting here talking about it and I'm not feeling a heck of a lot worse for it.

Next, competency-based counseling pastors need to *concentrate on actions and interactions rather than intrapsychic concepts.* To do this, the helper needs to focus on what is observable and describable rather than on what is unseen. The information to attend to is, therefore, "harder" than the internal processes of the "psyche" (such as those dreaded "drives" and "needs" that people believe so strongly in), and counseling can become more efficient because of this emphasis on pragmatic considerations.

Third, the way to influence the process of change in counseling is *to orient oneself toward tasks rather than toward insight.* Information (the "database") is thus pared down from all known and unknown internal processes to that which is most relevant on the road to problem resolution. Within our pastoral counseling model, insight is the result of change rather than the antecedent to it. (This will be addressed later in the chapter.)

JC: That's super, Walt. You know . . . now that I stop and think about it, I wonder what your wife would say is different when you are doing a little bit better?

W: Hmm . . . she might say that I am not in bed as much as usual or not as mopey to be around.

JC: OK. What else might she see you doing?

W: Dunno . . . no, don't have the foggiest.

JC: That's all right. Still, it could be interesting to see her response. Well, what if—this might sound like a crazy idea—what if we just pretend for a moment that you knew what else you might be doing . . . this is just pretending, OK? So, if your life was back on track, what would you be doing instead?

W: Shoot, that's easy. First, I wouldn't be walking around in this back brace all the time feeling like a cripple. Second, I'd be out looking for work at a job that paid decently. I couldn't get it any better than that, I mean, to get my self-esteem back.

JC: Which do you think is the more reasonable at this point?

W: Uh . . . I guess the easiest thing to do would be to make myself get up in the morning and do my exercises or walk on the treadmill like I am supposed to. See, it's like this: when I do the exercises I don't have to wear this brace as much, but when I get down in the dumps, the exercises and everything else don't matter.

JC: So, if I hear you right, you would start doing the exercises or walking on the treadmill?

W: Yeah, sure.

C: When you're out there walking or exercising, how will you keep track of your progress?

W: I have a spiral notebook that I used to keep around, but I'll probably have to go out and buy a new one.

Finally, *counseling needs to take a goal orientation*. This, along with the previous assumption, allows the helper and the counselee to form the end of this process as well as the beginning. If counseling has a target, you can know if you've hit it; if not, termination is indeterminable. "Long-term" counseling often removes the possibility of termination by focusing on character reformation or such global concepts as "mental health." If the road is labeled "normal," the destination is often so far away that it cannot be seen and remains unknown. This may also affect the ongoing relationship one wishes to maintain as a pastor or helper. It is easy to fall into a regular schedule of "pastoral care" or supportive ministry that could continue long after the presenting problem is resolved. Speaking openly about a goal for terminating "counseling" allows all parties to move toward a warm, pastoral relationship after the goal has been met and away from regularly scheduled sessions, creating more time for the helper to work with others who need intervention in the more formal counseling setting.

JC: Well, Walt, we've taken in a lot at this point. I wonder how you and I are going to know that we have been successful here?

W: I am not real sure. I guess that I won't get as easily discouraged about being out of work and not let it get the best of me.

JC: OK. What will the sign look like that says, "I'm not going to let it get the best of me"?

W: It would look like I will still be doing the exercise stuff and putting out feelers for some work. I've had a couple of offers but just couldn't seem to get it together.

JC: That's fine, Walt. Let me see if I have heard you right so far. You said that if you were to start exercising again you would not be very dependent on the brace. Of course, you preceded this, if I remember correctly, with the notion that you'd be out of bed, right?

W: Yep, that's it.

JC: Good. So one goal in coming here might be to simply monitor your progress and talk about how you continue to overcome the tendency to get discouraged during the process?

W: That'll work for me.

In summary, as you begin your journey, you need to get a useful map and get oriented. Our approach to pastoral counseling utilizes a map of counselee resourcefulness that emphasizes a narrow but relevant field of information, a concentration on that which is observable, an emphasis on tasks, and orientation toward an identifiable and achievable goal.

THE PRAGMATICS OF CHANGE: THE MAP "KEY" AND A MINIMUM OF TRAVEL INSTRUCTIONS[1]

Once you're oriented to the map, a knowledge of map "keys" will be helpful. These are kept to a minimum and are as pragmatic as possible in order to make identification easy and application simple. You could think of these as maxims, proverbs, shibboleths, or curb feelers—however you get a grasp on these, keep in mind that these will make following the map much easier than trying to read the map without them!

1. *If it works, don't fix it. If it doesn't, don't do more of it—do something different.* These two maxims, first developed by de Shazer (1985), are primary guides to doing brief pastoral counseling. First, one must learn to leave "well enough" alone. Attempts to improve what is an acceptable situation to the counselee can often lead to larger, more intractable problems. Since we helpers are charged to "do no harm" (Becvar, Becvar, and Bender 1982), pastoral counselors who believe they can "improve" a counselee should think about adopting this premise.

The other side of the coin is also indispensable. At the very least, realize that if you find yourself in a hole, you should stop digging! This concept is not new, as a number of counseling models emphasize this. It is phenomenal how many people attempt the same approach when it has failed over and over again—their determination is amazing! (By the way, this is as true for pastoral counselors as it is for counselees.) Helping people create new, viable approaches when their attempted solutions become part of the problem is a primary focus of our model of counseling.

I (FNT) had a seventeen-year-old counselee who had cut on himself to the extent that his mother and stepfather called the police for help. The police officer who responded happened to be a friend of the family, and he guided the family toward counseling instead of drastic measures such as involuntary hospitalization. When William and his mother came to the first session a few days after the cutting incident, I immediately saw that they neatly fell into Durrant's only diagnostic category—they were "stuck." Lila and William were locked in a struggle, and neither could get out of it. Lila continually asked William to talk to her about why he was cutting on himself. In response, William refused to speak. His refusal to talk, of course, led Lila to believe William *had* to tell her about his problems in order to get better, and she begged for him to tell her even more, which William, who did not believe talking would help, refused to do—a perfect example of interactional stuckness!

William would not tell me about his problems either, believing I was another adult who was "trying to get him to talk." Holding to the premise that one should not do more of what doesn't work, I struck a deal with the son and mother: if William would agree to come and see me for one session and continue *not* talking about his problems, then Lila would agree to back off and not ask William to tell her his problems. William left the session vowing *not* to talk about his problem, but promising to meet with me. Lila still had the right to seek police intervention if she felt her son was going to harm himself, and she promised to be vigilant yet silent.

About a week later, William came to my office and began to speak openly about his anger, destructive fighting, and self-cutting. I did not ask him to tell me about what he was experiencing, nor did I forbid it. My goal was twofold: (1) to stop the "digging" and (2) to make sure I did not pick up the shovel and repeat what was not working in this situation.

We met infrequently until William decided he had solved his problem and did not need to return. He found ways to "get his anger out," in his words, that were truly unique—and worked to his satisfaction. William no longer expressed his anger in destructive ways, for instead of harming himself or property, he chose to talk with an older male friend or simply to walk away from situations which used to provoke his anger. Although he continued to be selective with what he told his mother about his life, he no longer cut on himself and related that that particular behavior was no longer an option for him when he "got down." What is important to note is that William's problem was resolved to *his* satisfaction. There is no doubt in my mind that he could have changed other significant aspects of his life if he had continued in counseling; however, there is also no doubt in my mind that pushing him in this direction would have failed miserably, as he did not have any interest in becoming an honors student, growing closer to his mother, or working on areas of his life outside of "getting down." Three months after we completed counseling together, I contacted Lila by phone. She related that William is "the same old William, except he's not depressed anymore!" She no longer pushed him to tell her everything in his life, and they were getting along "like a normal adolescent and mom."

2. *Counselees, not pastors, are the experts on their lives and problems.* If you move from an "expert" stance to this position, your entire approach to pastoral counseling may change. Our approach assumes that counselees know much more about their lives and problems than we could ever learn, and since most pastoral counseling only lasts a few weeks, it is imperative that we put people in charge of their change immediately and avoid the trap of taking over as an expert.

This is especially important to keep in mind during the goal-setting stage of counseling. The belief that counselees have not only the right but the ability to decide what is best for them should be written at the top of every note you take! Goal setting, however, is not a passive exercise for the helper.

3. *A focus on the possible and changeable is more helpful than a focus on the overwhelming and intractable.* When setting goals with counselees, it is imperative that you, the helper, keep the goals in the range of the reasonable. This is not the same as "realistic"; in our experience, most counselees change beyond our expectations and predictions, thus poking holes in our ideas of "realistic" on a regular basis. Focusing on the possible requires consideration of the following ideas:

- Can the counselee be on track toward this goal in a short period of time?
- Is this goal verifiable by anyone but the counselee?
- Is it achievable, given this person's successful past experiences?
- Is any movement toward this goal under the control of the counselee?

For example, Rhoda comes to see you for pastoral counseling. It is immediately obvious that Rhoda has very strong ideas about what counseling should focus on. She states that her husband, Ron, has been neglectful of her to the point where she is considering a trial separation in the near future. In the first few minutes, Rhoda states her goal as "getting Ron to shape up." By comparing Rhoda's initial (rough-draft) goal with the above criteria, one can quickly see that this goal would not fit within the limits of this approach to pastoral counseling. This is not to say that Rhoda could not have this as a goal in life or in another counseling setting—this goal simply cannot be achieved by Rhoda, nor would the most of the movement toward it be under her control. Getting Ron to "shape up" would mostly fall under Ron's agency or control, not Rhoda's. Also, this goal is amorphous, making it almost impossible to be verified by anyone but Rhoda.

Within this model, Rhoda's initial idea needs modification in order for her to work toward it, know when she's on track, and be able to have both outside verification and personal control. Here is a possible adjustment that could be negotiated between you and Rhoda: First, she needs to identify what she would call her experience when Ron was "not being neglectful," placing this experience in positive terms so that the presence of the appropriate and pleasant could be increased (instead of having less of the "neglectful" behavior) (see Berg and Miller 1992). Let's say that Rhoda redefines what she wants from Ron as "paying attention to me" instead of "not being neglectful." There— done, right? No! Here's the hard part: we *still* don't know what this is! Many people proceed in counseling under what Weiner-Davis (1992) calls "the Immaculate Assumption." Until you and Rhoda share (aloud) descriptions of interactions and observable actions that would exemplify "paying attention to me," you simply cannot know what it is. Also, it is difficult to increase one's control over this or verify its presence without careful articulation of examples. By probing for actions and interactions that would give evidence *to her* that Ron is "paying attention to her" (see "miracle question" below), Rhoda gives the following initial list:

- he asks her how her day went;
- he initiates talking with her;
- he tells her what he appreciates about her.

Now you and Rhoda can work on setting a goal for your time together. Even though all of the above examples involve Ron's behavior, they are easily formed into measurable goals with specific outcome so that everyone involved—you, Rhoda, and Ron—can verify changes taking place. Also, although a great deal of this initial goal idea is dependent on Ron's change, Rhoda's part in the change process can now be addressed in several ways. First, you could ask Rhoda if she does these particular things herself! Also, Rhoda could be asked to identify present examples of when Ron *does* initiate conversation, ask her about her day, or other closely related behaviors. Rhoda could also examine her role in making such expectations clear to Ron: Has she verbalized these desires to him? Is she sure he is able to respond to her requests? What part has she played to create the opportunity for these changes to happen? That is, do they see each other enough to raise such topics, and does she allow him to talk when they are together? All of these approaches could be related to Rhoda's desire for change, with the forming of counseling goals focused on that which is feasible.

The possible and changeable may be evident in the present experience of the counselee and in the future. We will outline below ways of channeling your natural curiosity through presuppositional, future-oriented questions in order to bring the possible and changeable to the forefront.

4. *Every complaint description includes some sort of exception.* Our assumption is that nothing happens 100 percent of the time—there are always exceptions to the normal pattern of a problem. To quote de Shazer (1988, 4):

> The term *exception* is used because clients tend to view their complaints or problems as "always happening" (a rule). When the complaint does not happen, it is as if a rule had been broken but that change is not seen as significant. The non-occurrence of the problem is seen as "a fluke" rather than as evidence that things might be getting better, suggesting that "every rule has an exception."

The way to identify exceptions (de Shazer et al. 1986) is to focus on two things: competence and difference.

A man in his late thirties placed a call early one morning to the church secretary to make an appointment for counseling with Jack. What was out of the ordinary was the man's reluctance either to give either his name or to explain why he had to have a male counselor.

JC: Hi, I'm Jack. The secretary said she didn't have your name.
K: Ken.
JC: Well, Ken, would you like to tell me what has been going on in your life that relates to us meeting here?
K: I'm not real sure where to start. I drive around the city a lot because I'm a sales rep and I've been making great money. But last week the police came by the office and were questioning me about something that happened on the freeway.
JC: OK, I'm all ears.
K: Well, you see, I'm driving around the freeway in my Mercedes and I see an attractive woman. Well. I basically masturbate until

she sees what I'm doing. I know, I know . . . that sounds sick, but lately I can't get sex off my mind. You know, all the time, I mean, even to the point of doing it in the car six, maybe seven times a day. Jeez, I feel guilty like God is really going to get me for this.

JC: Excuse me for asking, but how did the police find you?

K: The last woman had a car phone and called in my license plate. What's worse is them calling my house and talking to my wife about it!

JC: Have you spoken to her about it?

K: Not a word. Don't have to. She thinks I'm sick just because I keep a few magazines around.

JC: OK, so what's going to be useful for me to know about this situation?

K: It's gotten out of control. I mean, this masturbation stuff is going to get me into deep water real quick. I'm worried that I won't be able to stop and that I'll get busted. To tell you the truth, sometimes it feels like a possession or something.

JC: When was the last time you were able to overcome the temptation to give in?

K: I've never been able not to. Once I see the woman clearly it's too late.

JC: What do you mean, "clearly"?

K: Well, in order to get started I need to see their faces as if there was nothing between us.

JC: When was there a time, say, when less than optimal conditions were sufficient for you not to give in?

K: Oh, that happens all the time.

JC: So unless it's, say, clear, absolutely clear, you can control the tendency to give in?

K: Nine times out of ten, you bet.

JC: OK, Ken, at this point I'm thinking window blocks, you know, the legal limit for tinting.

Although this may seem like an example of extreme pathology, Ken reported that he no longer masturbates in public and pointed out the direct connection between the tinting and the change. Since he was no longer making eye contact, the cycle was interrupted. A three-month follow-up found Ken and his wife working on their own marital problems in a productive way and no additional brushes with the law.

5. *The pastor's job is to be respectfully curious whenever possible.* This final idea has opened new vistas for us. Our focus has moved away from pathological labels, struggling for control, and strategic game-playing toward an approach marked by respect and curiosity. We believe that if one holds to these ideas, then cooperation and positive change follows.

In our approach, one's curiosity is guided by the desire to know more about the counselee's experience of the problem and its context. Knowing the influence of the problem from the counselee's viewpoint allows the pastor to search for exceptions and resources, and soliciting information with respectful questions gives the pastoral counselor more room to maneuver. We have found that this particular approach is more than a method as it creates space for the relentless optimism and abundant references to hidden resources that this model requires for success.

Now, with this map key and set of instructions in hand, we would like to direct you to the final piece that currently informs our approach in counseling—the map itself.[2]

A MAP FOR COMPETENCY-BASED COUNSELING

When choosing a map for counseling, one must make sure that the map fits with the assumptions, procedures, and goals of one's approach. Our map, based on one developed by Michael Durrant and Kate Kowalski (1993), has proven to be a useful guide to those working within competency-based assumptions. No map is perfect—it is simply the pastoral counselor's tool to guide you when you're lost, to show you when you're on the right track, and to lead you toward effective work with people.

Use this map for comparison as you read the following descriptions, as these descriptions outline the category boxes on the map. All the reading in the world will not help you become an artful, effective pastoral counselor. But if you have no practical guidance, you won't know how to implement the ideas of the model. So, the questions we have given as examples need to be tailored to your own vocabulary, congregation, culture, and so on. Keep in mind that this is a question-driven approach—counselees are the experts on their lives, so the information required for change does not come from the pastoral counselor but from the life experiences of the counselees.

A MAP FOR
COMPETENCY-BASED COUNSELING

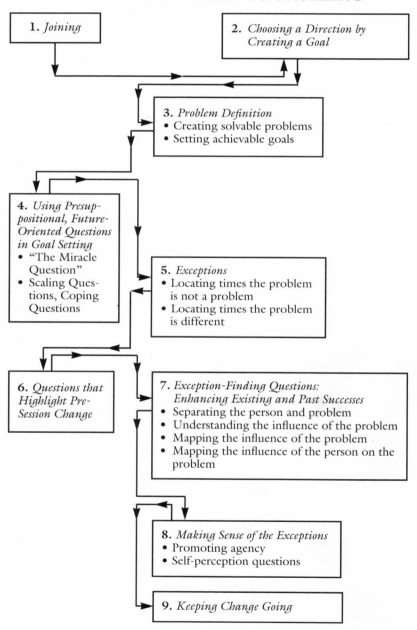

1. *Joining*

2. *Choosing a Direction by Creating a Goal*

3. *Problem Definition*
- Creating solvable problems
- Setting achievable goals

4. *Using Presuppositional, Future-Oriented Questions in Goal Setting*
- "The Miracle Question"
- Scaling Questions, Coping Questions

5. *Exceptions*
- Locating times the problem is not a problem
- Locating times the problem is different

6. *Questions that Highlight Pre-Session Change*

7. *Exception-Finding Questions: Enhancing Existing and Past Successes*
- Separating the person and problem
- Understanding the influence of the problem
- Mapping the influence of the problem
- Mapping the influence of the person on the problem

8. *Making Sense of the Exceptions*
- Promoting agency
- Self-perception questions

9. *Keeping Change Going*

BOX #1: Joining with the Counselee(s)

The first step was what counted. Once you've begun a thing,
it exercises a terrible authority over you.

—Jules Romain

Every model of counseling addresses the idea of "joining." We use the term "joining" to mean the actions, words, and contextual cues used by the helper to establish a positive counseling relationship. Many counseling approaches assume that without proper joining with the counselees, progress will not be achieved. We hold to the idea that, as a pastor, you have the requisite skills to put people at ease and create a safe environment for important conversation. So, do what you usually do to create a context open to change.

In keeping with the assumptions of our model of pastoral counseling, an important feature of joining could be called "socializing." Instead of establishing a relationship based on hierarchy (the Tarzan Approach: "Me pastor, you counselee"), our approach to joining attempts to build a more collaborative relationship and encourage the contributions of the counselee(s). By thinking of the beginning of a session as socializing, you can begin this relationship on the right track toward competent living.

It really is quite simple: *when joining, ask about success.* Whenever possible, begin the initial contact and subsequent sessions by asking about success-possible topics such as occupation, interests, hobbies, school, friends, and so on. One guiding idea might be: if you are fairly sure the counselee can answer your question with something positive, go ahead and ask it. Here are a few of our favorite introductory questions:

- So, now that I have everyone's name down, what do you do for fun?
- John, what do you enjoy in life?
- Mary, what do you like about your daughter, Susan?
- Bill, so you're a carpenter. Tell me a little about that. What are you particularly good at? What part of carpentry do you enjoy the most?
- So, Lori, what's your favorite subject in school? Tell me what you enjoy about it.

The result of directing questions and imperatives like these toward your counselees is usually the creation of a relaxed atmosphere that is focused on competency and resources *from the very start*. We have found that beginning each case (and each session) with "competency talk" generates a natural transition to competency talk around the presenting problem, exceptions, and goals. Feedback from counselees who have worked with us is clear: this approach leads people to believe that there is more to them than their problem. Pastoral counselors who ask about other, successful aspects of counselees' lives will confirm that the counselees *are* more than their problems.

BOX #2: Choosing a Direction by Creating a Goal

If your train is on the wrong track, every station you come to is the wrong station.
                                                                —Bernard Malamud

Most people who come to counseling have preconceptions of what will take place. Whether they gleaned these ideas from watching old television reruns such as "The Bob Newhart Show," listening to others' descriptions of their counseling, or past personal experience, one aspect of success in all counseling is the meeting of counselees' expectations regarding what should happen in the counseling room (Miller et al., 1995). Most people expect to relate their experiences around the problem, pain, or dilemma confronting them. Some models of brief counseling (see de Shazer, 1988) spend a minimum amount of time on what has come to be known as "problem talk"; however, in our experience, people in counseling need to express themselves regarding their reason(s) for coming. At this stage, you can invite the persons to tell their stories, keeping in mind that the accounts will change from that moment on because of you, the telling of the story, and the questions you raise. Remember, nothing stays the same; change is inevitable.

Here are some questions that may help in the transition to this stage:

- Well, what do I need to know about your coming here?
- What do you think would be helpful for me to know?
- What is the most important thing I need to know about your situation?
- Please describe what has been happening related to why you're here today.

Notice that this invitation is open to both problem talk and competency talk. If a counselee responds to the question, "What do you think would be helpful for me to know?" he or she could talk about problematic circumstances, personal anguish, past successes, or helpful friends and still be responding appropriately.

If you were to ask, "What is the problem?" you might create two difficult situations. First, if more than one person is in the room, each may believe that his or her story is the most correct version. If you've done any pastoral counseling with couples, you have heard exchanges like this:

Husband: I got in at about the usual time—
Wife: It was 6:30—*way* past when he said he would
           come home—
Husband: It was *not* 6:30; it was more like 6:15—
Wife: (*Interrupts, offers a conflicting view.*)

Once people begin to compete for the position of "the truth," it can be difficult to steer discussion toward more helpful conversation.

Second, asking about the problem can reify or solidify the problem's position in the context. We have found that people will discuss their experiences of the problem(s) and their uncertainties about its form if asked more open questions about their experiences. As you follow the map further, you will see where this is going. The problem will usually be reformulated in a more positive, hopeful form, either because those present experience the problem differently or because its original presentation did not allow for solutions. (More on that later.)

It is important to get each person's view of the problem. Every person's viewpoint will differ because every person is different. Our friends in law enforcement have often told us that they know there is something amiss when all the witnesses tell the same story, because human beings bring unique viewpoints to every experience. When counselees share information, it is important that the pastor *pay attention to each counselee's language*. We have found that if we utilize the counselees' understanding and experience of their problems and resources from the beginning of counseling, we are more productive and effectual. Remembering the assumption that "the counselee is the expert on his or her life and experience," we try to fit into the vocabulary and style of self-description whenever possible. After all, the pastor should be the flexible one in this context—it will be much easier for you to adapt than for the counselee to transform his or her language of description. (Each helper's personal sense of decency should dictate flexibility, of course.)

For example: William's description of his problem included the phrase "pissed off." Although this may not be a preferred, socially acceptable form of description, I (FNT) adopted his phrase as an apt description of his feelings. Instead of attempting to get William to use more clinically accurate or socially acceptable words like "angry" or "frustrated," I simply adapted to his description and worked on exceptions to, behavioral descriptions of, and goals regarding this state of being "pissed off."

Our counseling experience tells us that the most important aspect of doing efficient and effective pastoral counseling involves the setting of a goal. Following the lead of the socializing stage, the next aspect of the counseling session involves goal setting. As discussed above, the pastor's aim is to cocreate a solvable problem *with* the counselee(s), not for them.

BOX #3: Problem Definition:
Creating Solvable Problems and Setting Achievable Goals

J. W. Getzels wrote an article years ago entitled "The Problem of the Problem" (Getzels 1982), in which he relates a story about two cars traveling a deserted highway. The first car happens to hit a small obstruction that punctures a tire. Upon pulling off the road and examining the situation, the driver of this car opens the trunk to pull out the car jack, only to find that the jack is missing. The problem for this driver is posed: "Where can I get a jack?" With the problem formed in this way, he begins the long walk toward the nearest town, hoping to locate a jack with which to change the tire. The second car hits the same obstacle with the same result—a punctured tire. Upon discovering that she also has no jack in the trunk of the car, she reforms her question. Instead of asking "Where can I get a jack?" she poses her problem in the following form: "How can *I raise the car?*" Looking about her, she discovers a barn just off the road. In the barn loft is a block and tackle used to raise hay into the loft. She utilizes this block and tackle to raise the car, changes the tire, and drives on her way. Hopefully, the man walking down the lonely stretch of highway caught a ride with her! Getzels' point must be taken to heart by those attempting to utilize our model of counseling: *problems must be fashioned into solvable forms toward which the counselee(s) can work.* Without this important step, pastoral counseling will simply become an exercise of floundering and frustration for you and the counselees.

We believe that re-forming a problem into a solvable form involves several qualities, all of which are negotiable with the counselee. Borrowing from Berg and Miller (1992), these qualities are:

1. *Saliency to the counselee(s).*

Every goal must be important to the problem(s) brought to the counseling setting. Although the pastor may have ideals or ideas about what underlies the problem, the counselee is the final judge of its relevance. For example, because of prior training in psychodynamic theory, Dr. Jones believes that Dave's problem of "impotence" is based on a deep-seated, unconscious fear of castration. To Dave, this is pure mumbo-jumbo—he simply wants to be able to maintain an erection when making love with his wife. To Dr. Smith, who had structural family therapy training, Billy's tantrums are simply a symptom of a dysfunctional marital relationship between Neil and Lois, and the real change needs to take place in the marital subsystem. Neither of these approaches is wrong; that is, in another model, the hypotheses presented by Drs. Jones and Smith would fit well with the procedure outlined in their respective theoretical "maps." It is doubtful, however, that the counselees in these situations would think their explanations to be reasonable; without the background theory, neither of these "problems," as re-formed by the helper, would make sense or be salient to the counselee(s).

Following the idea of Pascal stated at the beginning of this chapter, the counselee is much more likely to move toward a goal that he or she believes is relevant to solving the problem at hand. If a person wants to cut down on smoking, then the goal could be to "cut down on smoking"! According to this model of pastoral counseling, goals regarding problems such as "I want to be more outgoing," "I need to control my temper better," or "I have a fear of test-taking" would find the respective re-formed goals of "becoming more outgoing," "controlling my temper better," and "managing my test-taking fear" more relevant.

2. *Small.*

Weiner-Davis and others support the idea that people would rather reach small goals often than achieve lofty, lifelong dreams occasionally.

In translating this to the pastoral counseling setting, we need to nego-
tiate goals with counselees that are *attainable*. A large number of cases
fail because, to borrow a metaphor from pole vaulting, "the bar is set
too high." In our training sessions, we often use a cartoon illustration
that pictures a mother reading a fairy tale aloud to her daughter at bed-
time. The caption reads, "So the prince and the princess lowered their
expectations and lived reasonably contentedly forever after!" Success in
our model of pastoral counseling—or most counseling—is tied to
motivation, and one of the best motivators is the continuous achievement of goals.

Questions such as these illustrate the concept:

- What will be a small sign that you have moved toward your goal?
- If you were to make a small step toward change, what would that
  look like?
- I think your goal of _____ is well stated. If you were on
  your way toward this goal, what would be the first thing _____
  (your mother, your daughter, your boss) might notice you doing
  differently?

The emphasis resides with language around the first and not the
final thing you would see. Giving change a foothold is often as simple
as "lowering the bar" to the point that the counselee(s) cannot help
but see change happening in their lives. Remember: if you continue to
fail, lower your standards!

3. *Concrete, specific, and behavioral.*

Goals for pastoral counseling are best formed in ways that can be verified by others. This is not to negate the importance of that which cannot be seen (such as cognitive or affective change, differences in motivation, and so on); instead, it is formed on the premise that change leads
to more change (the "snowball effect"). That is, we firmly believe that
people's motives, emotions, and cognitions will change as they experience positive difference in their problems at a behavioral and interactional level. Others, including William Powers, Howard Stone, and
William Glasser, have written about this position and guided helpers
toward models that focus on behavioral change. It is not necessary to
change one aspect of one's life first; counseling models abound, and
whether they place affect, cognition, or behavior as antecedent to further change, all models have followers and all produce change.

In our model of pastoral counseling, elusive and vague goals are more difficult to work toward than those formed in concrete, verifiable terms. It is simply easier for the counselee to report changes such as, "I got out of the house three times this week" as indicators of change than it is to measure "happier" or "less depressed." "The advantage of defining goals in precise terms is that it becomes easier for the therapist and counselee to evaluate exactly what progress is being made, as well as to determine what else remains to be accomplished" (Berg and Miller 1992, 37). Here are some examples that illustrate the concept: being to work on time three out of five days this week; controlling my temper with little Nicole 75 percent of the time; looking in the want ads to locate job opportunities every day; making four calls on new people to generate new business; going to two church functions and sitting by someone I don't know; and so on.

We believe that it is important to attend to the counselee's total experience, and that one's emotional state and responses are paramount in the counseling process. Although we emphasize behavioral and interactional features in goal setting, we do not exclude the affective from any aspect of this approach[3] (Lipchik 1993). According to Harré and Secord (1972, 272), "an emotion is roughly the *meaning* we give our felt states of arousal [emphasis added] and is therefore ever-changing rather than a fact." There is a firm body of evidence that supports the idea that "self-attribution of emotion is related to the way we make sense of what we observe in our own behavior" (Cade and O'Hanlon 1993, 46f), and this model emphasizes those parts of experience which can be attained and observed more than other aspects of experience. In our practices, we have noticed that counselees express emotion differently when we use the CBC approach. In addition to the pain, confusion, and anxiety that often accompanies the relating of problem stories, we have also seen emotional expressions of joy, relief, and determination, leading us to believe that a competency-based approach allows for a broader range of counselee experience than models that place primary emphasis on cathartic, behavioral, or problem-focused experience. Please keep in mind that paying attention to certain aspects of the counseling experience does not negate other important facets—we are simply working more with those portions of experience most easily addressed in the goal-oriented change process.

4. *Presence rather than the absence of something.*

In competency-based counseling, goals cannot be stated in the negative. To be "less depressed" is possible, but it continually focuses on the negative past rather than on the future, positive goal. That is, focusing on being "less depressed" is still focusing on depression. "Paradox . . . results whenever we try to tell ourselves *not* to do something. That is, whenever we tell ourselves to *not* do something we are forced to think about the very activity that we are supposed to avoid" (Berg and Miller 1992, 39). One should redefine or create the counselee's goal in a hopeful, positively directed form. Therefore, we often ask our counselees what they would be doing or feeling, or what they hope to be doing or feeling *instead*.

It is best to work with the counselee to form ideas about what to call the goal when the problem involves reducing or eliminating an unwanted experience. Using "depression" as an example, one might ask, "What would you be experiencing if your depression disappeared?" Or, "What would you call the opposite of 'depression'?" The following terms have been coined by counselees as the opposite, positive experience: "up," "confident," "jovial," "content," "happy," and "at peace." Beginning from "depression" and moving to "happy" creates the possibility of a target to aim at (and, consequently, to hit).

Here are a few other examples of recreated problems:

Rather than:	Use:
I'm depressed	I need to be more content
I'm afraid I backslid	I need to seek forgiveness, grow closer to God
We don't communicate	We need to communicate better
We want to stop fighting	We need to have more pleasant times together
We've got to stop our crazy binge spending	We need to get better control of our finances

5. *Beginning rather than an end.*

The greatest temptation of any goal setting is to focus on the point of ultimate success. Within our model of counseling, clients and helpers need to pay careful attention to the first, small step of the process of change. Since the focus of our model of pastoral counseling is success, it is best to identify the first step toward the perfect solution when working with people who come to you for help.

With one couple a wonderful metaphor was created that illustrates the importance of this concept. Glenda and Gary, who had been married six years, were best friends as well as lovers. Their sex life, however, was less than satisfying for both of them (but for different reasons). Gary was an engineer who believed "good sex" could be achieved by creating a plan, breaking it down into its component parts, and following it step by step to completion (much like creating and following a blueprint!). Glenda believed in a "state" of perfect sex, one that could not be achieved but would "just happen, if it did happen." Needless to say, they were very stuck when they first came to counseling! The first three sessions were spent creating a goal that everyone—counselor included—could understand and work with. To everyone's surprise, the fourth session was the last—the formation of a beginning was the end of formal counseling! Here's the conversation that led to the mutual decision to "go it on (their) own":

Glenda: When we first came in, I thought I could see over the horizon. I mean, I already knew what "perfect sex" would be. Now—

Gary: Now, neither of us knows what that will be like. When we were with others [past lovers], we knew . . . but great sex with them might not be great sex with each other!

FT: So, how will you know you're headed in the right direction?

Glenda: I think we know the direction (*looking at Gary, who nods*) . . . we're just in a fog and can only see about a foot in front of us—

Gary: —but we're holding hands, walking in the fog together for the first time. We've been talking and we don't think we need to come back anymore.

FT: Sounds like you know where you're going—

Glenda: And when we get there, it probably won't be anything like what I "knew" it was! Now, I'm sure it's over the horizon.

FT: It might be better!

Gary: Well, it'll be a fun trip!

6. *Realistic and achievable within the context of the counselee's life.*

The heroine in Eleanor Porter's novel *Pollyanna* was foolishly optimistic, which resulted in some difficult predicaments for her. Competency-based counseling can appear "Pollyann-ish" to some helpers and counselees because of its relentless optimism and orientation away from pathology and problems. It is not our intent to plunge into this any-thing-is-possible trap. At the same time, "being realistic" can potential-ly limit change more than anything else we can imagine when employ-ing this model. Helpers often view people and situations as having unavoidable, inherent barriers, to the point that they believe these views are factual. The helper must practice careful distinctions between what is fact ("Spinach is green") and what is opinion ("Spinach is good").

In order to avoid the Pollyanna Pitfall and still work within what Bill O'Hanlon calls "PossibilityLand" (O'Hanlon and Beadle 1994), a context must be created that allows for dreaming without ignoring facts and that takes into account what is achievable in the life of the counselee. Sometimes it is best to talk about what is *not* within the con-trol of the counselee and move toward what lies within the person's sphere of control. For example, one father came to counseling with the goal to "get my adolescent son to stop thinking about sex" (yes, it's true!). This is clearly outside of the father's control and needs to be addressed as such.

Often, counselees come with goals that focus on "never" or "always," and one can clearly predict failure when the future depends on perfection. If someone says, "My goal is never, ever to lose my tem-per with my daughter again!" the helper can steer the discussion toward an achievable goal in two ways. First, one needs to question the reality of complete control of one's temper. It is clear to most human beings that no one is in perfect control of anything, and most counse-lees quickly pick up on the imminent failure of such a goal (especially when the helper uses a bit of humor and self-disclosure to point this out: "Well, when you discover how to do that, let me know so we can bottle it and make a million!"). Second, through the use of scaling (see below), both the first steps toward better temper control and an acceptable level of control can be discussed. For example:

FNT: OK, you'd like to have perfect control over your temper,
           so would I. If "perfect control" was a "10" and "out of
           control" is a "0," what would you settle for and still say
           you've done well?
Counselee: I think I'd like to have a "10."

FNT: Everyone would; but, let's assume you're human for the time being, and hitting a "10" just isn't possible for you and me. What would be an acceptable level of control, on a scale from 0 to 10?

Counselee: Well, maybe an "8."

FNT: And where are you now, today?

Counselee: Maybe a "4."

FNT: How does that compare to where you were on your worst day last week?

Counselee: Oh, I'm sure I was around a "2" last Thursday.

FNT: So, you've already made some steps toward that "8." What did you do to make that happen?

Staying realistic and moving toward achievable goals keeps counseling focused on a target that doesn't move or change shape. Taking steps forward only count when both the client and pastoral counselor believe these steps are in a direction that will help momentum to build.

7. Perceived as involving "hard work."

One of the most important lessons I (FNT) have learned in my years of competency-based counseling and supervision involves "saving face." Because of my contact with many Asian counselors-in-training, I have come to see the importance of creating choices with counselees (and helpers) that allow them to maintain their dignity. Any simpleton can point out the obvious: "You messed up!" Since this model is focused on the creation of respectful relationships and successful experiences, however, we believe in promoting dignity. One of the easiest ways to achieve this is to frame any success as involving "hard work." As Berg and Miller (1992, 43) state, "Failure only means more hard work remains to be done, not that the client cannot accomplish her (or his) goal." In fact, framing past failures as a result of encountering a particularly difficult problem means that failures are expected and are not to be attributed to the counselee's personality, intelligence, or history.

We have found that most tasks can be prefaced with the phrase, *"Most people would find this difficult to do, but, this week . . . "* This idea usually allows the person to maintain dignity no matter what the outcome. If the counselee does not successfully complete the task, then she or he can be seen as "just like most people" when faced with this

difficult problem. Failure to create positive change can be dismissed—
"Well, no problem; most people have a difficult time with it." On the
other hand, if things go well and positive change is noted, then he or
she can be viewed as unusually successful. We often say, "Since most
people find changing this way difficult, how were you able to accomplish it?" As you can imagine, optimism remains high when "win-win"
outcomes are created.

In chapter 4, we move to the pragmatic aspects of this approach,
giving the reader multiple examples of questions and responses that
will help you ease into a competency orientation. We have found that
jumping into the competency approach is as easy as the "fear and trepidation" approach for most pastors. Either way, you have the concepts
. . . next, the examples.

4

A MAP FOR COMPETENCY-BASED COUNSELING
Part II: Getting on the (Short) Road to Change

Continuing the themes of chapter 3, here we provide multiple examples of our competency-based approach. We hope the categories clarify the map from chapter 3 and that the case examples illuminate the process. One hint as you begin: We have found that memorizing some interventive questions from each category makes trying out the model much, much simpler. We memorized questions from Weakland, White, de Shazer, and Berg in our learning over the past decade and have found that memorizing questions allows one to focus on the content and the *process* of the session because one does not have to form queries from scratch each time.

Some may believe that this mapped-out approach is too confining and predictable for both the counseling pastor and those attending the sessions. We have found comfort in the structure, knowing that the road we are taking has been effective for many thousands of clients, even if it appears to be a bit predictable. One example: My (FNT) daughter went through my learning with me, as many families do. I admit that I have incorporated many of these ideas into my daily approach to enhancing relationships and solving problems. One day, as I was carefully listening to Allison articulate a problem she was having with people at school, I opened my mouth to respond. Before I could, she replied in a singsong voice, "I know, I know, Dad—'When doesn't this happen?'" (She went on to solve her own problem!) You see, even knowing how this approach works and what might be said next doesn't negate its effectiveness.

Now, back to our map . . .

BOX #4: Using Presuppositional, Future-Oriented Questions in Goal Setting

The map illustrated in chapter 3 allows for a short trip on a "sidetrack" when goal formation gets stuck on past problems and failure. A keystone in forming goals is the use of questions that presuppose change. Keeping with the tenet that one's language is important, the helper's questions need to assume positive outcome for the counselee(s). Helpers aid in the goal-setting process by anticipating success from the beginning of counseling, and one of the easiest and most effective means to this end is forming questions that assume the problem will be resolved. Here are some examples:

- Let's make a leap of faith and say that our session ends up being helpful for you; how will you know?
- You seem like an optimist, so let's assume that you're able to beat the problem. What do you imagine will be different for you?
- "Between now and the next time we meet, I would like you to observe, so you can describe to me next time, what happens in your (pick one: family, life, marriage, relationship) that you want to continue to have happen." (de Shazer 1985, 137).

Walter and Peller (1992) talk about the importance of the words we use to set a climate for change. They emphasize words such as "yet" and "will," "when" and "so far" as examples of anticipatory language. Some examples:

Rather than:	Use:
It's never happened	It's never happened *yet*, but . . .
It's never happened	*So far* it hasn't happened, but . . .
If you	*When* you . . .
What have you done to	What *will* you be doing *when* . . .

Presuppositional Questions: The Miracle Question

When setting the agenda for pastoral counseling, for us the most powerful tool to date seems to be "the miracle question" (de Shazer 1988). A creation of de Shazer and his associates at the Brief Family Therapy Center in Milwaukee based on Milton Erickson's "crystal ball technique" (see de Shazer 1978), this particular approach to goal formation helps place the counselee in a future context in which the prob-

lem is not dominating his or her life. We have found that most counselees who have difficulty setting positive goals have never envisioned the
future without the problem—in short, the idea of a future without the
problem has never been considered! In fact, their "stuck" view of the
situation has led to an *inability* to foresee a future without the problem. To create hope and positive expectations, we would suggest that
the helper tailor-make a question along the lines of "the miracle question" or "the video description question." When we began working
within this model of counseling, we simply memorized one or the
other and asked it verbatim of each and every counselee. This practice
led to more efficient goal setting, heightened awareness of future possibilities, and the discovery of new resources for solving the problem,
all in a few minutes' time! Here they are:

THE MIRACLE QUESTION

"If a miracle were to happen tonight while you were asleep and tomor-
row morning you awoke to find that this problem were no longer a part
of your life, what would be different? What would be the first small thing
that will indicate to you that this miracle had taken place? How would
other people be able to tell without you telling them?" (de Shazer et al.
1986).

VIDEO DESCRIPTION QUESTION

"If I had two video tapes, one of you when you are standing up to the
influence of the problem, and another when the problem is getting the
best of you, what would I notice about the one where you are in charge?
What would I notice that's different about you in that video?" or "Let's
say that we have two video tapes of you, one is in the past when the
problem was really getting in the way for you and the other is sometime
in the near future when things are better. What's most noticeable in the
tape of you in the future that will tell us that things are better for you?"
(see O'Hanlon and Wilk 1987).

Utilizing these questions and others like them encourages counselees to think of a future without the problem, perhaps for the first time
in their lives (O'Hanlon and Weiner-Davis 1989). We have found that
simply asking the miracle question has led to profound changes in the
counselee's level of hope (see Lester 1995) as well as in the envisioning
of goals that could lead to a life not dominated by the problem. This
shift in possibilities is essential to change within our model of counseling, for it will allow the formation of meaningful goals with the coun-

selee that are in line with both the elimination (or minimization) of the experienced problem and the idealized life the counselee would like to lead. To remain consistent with the needs and values of the person seeking help, both goal achievement and sensitivity to a person's specific needs and dreams are crucial.

Presuppositional Questions: Scaling Questions
Change is often easier both to conceptualize and to achieve when it is removed from the all/nothing dichotomy. The method called "scaling" (Berg and Miller 1992, Kowalski and Kral 1989) has become one of the most widely used methods of creating an environment that encourages small steps toward a goal and allows both counselee(s) and helper to trace progress in a somewhat tangible way.

Berg and Miller (1992) see it this way:

> There is magic in numbers. When the client is asked to put his problems, priorities, successes, emotional investments in relationships, and level of self-esteem on a numerical scale, it gives the therapist a much better assessment of the things he has to know. . . . The scaling questions are designed to inform the therapist and are also used to motivate, encourage, and enhance the change process (pp. 82-83).

Here is a generic scaling question, which we encourage you to adapt to your particular style of curiosity:
On a scale from 0 to 10, where "10" means the best things could ever be, and "0" means the worst things have been, where would you say you are right now? (adopted from Durrant 1995, 46).

Counselees often want to reach a "10" before they feel they have accomplished their counseling goal. We believe that adopting a scale on which "10" is not achievable allows both the pastor and the counselee(s) to succeed before the problem is completely solved (if it can be). Similarly, "0" is used because clients will sometimes rate themselves at a "1" but almost never rate themselves as "0" (Durrant 1996).

The use of scaling questions allows everyone involved to have a unique experience of progress toward goals. Often, couples differ when they scale their progress during a session—whether it is "trust," "communication," or other amorphous problems (in fact, we have had couples argue about whether it was "really" an "8" or a "5"!). The fact of the matter is, this is not about facts! Change—be it toward one end of the scale or the other—is what is important, and the particular changes that people make to effect change are paramount.

Here are a few examples of how we have used the scaling technique in ways that are meaningful to counselees as well as pastoral counselors:

- On a scale of 0 to 10, with "0" being the worst your _____ (counselee's word) has ever been and "10" being the best you could hope for, where is it for you today? Follow with: What number would you have to reach in order to say that counseling with me has been successful?

- OK, I know you'd like to be at a "10." But let's say that "10" is perfection, and you're ready to move toward that "10" this week in a small way. What would you have to do to get it from the current "3" to, say, a "4"?

- OK, so your trust is at a "4" today. When you're able to say it's at a "5" or "6" (add 1 or 2 to the counselee's response), what will you be doing differently?"

- For children: I would like for you to rate your _____ (counselee's word) each day. Mom, I would like for you to rate his ____ each day, also. Don't tell each other what your rating is, but keep track of it and we'll talk about it next time. (This often highlights the child as expert of her or his own problem, since Mom will be "wrong" on her rating of the "actual rating number" of the child nearly every time.)

- So your _____ (counselee's word) has improved from a "2" to a "4." What did you do to move up from "2" to "4" in such a short time?

- What would it take to get the problem from a "5" to a "6"?

Presuppositional Questions: Coping Questions

Every helper has moments of fascination as well as frustration. One of our experiences of *both* happens when someone repeatedly says that his or her problem is "as bad as always" (or some derivative)! Some problems are so overwhelming that it is difficult for the person to notice positive change or influence over the problem. Counselees who have suffered a terrific loss and those who have been experiencing depression or suicidal thoughts often believe that the problem is never "better," and attempts to "get them to see" exceptions are frustrating and potentially harmful for the counselee.

At these moments, we switch to a form of questioning around the person's coping abilities. At any given moment, we firmly believe that *people are doing the best they can.* This does not mean that they are always succeeding; to the contrary, many times they are simply trying to keep their heads above water . . . but, they *are* succeeding at this, or they would not make the counseling session! Rather than minimizing problems or creating anxiety around failure, we refocus on competence. The following questions may be helpful in guiding you toward individualized questions that highlight competency in coping:

- *So right now, you just "barely cope"* (counselee's words). *What do you do to 'barely cope' each day?*
- *How do you keep going every day?*
- *How did you manage to get up this morning?*
- *So you thought seriously of killing yourself* (counselee's words). *How did you manage to get to this session?*
- *So the problem isn't any better. Often, problems get worse with time . . . What have you been doing to keep the problem from getting any worse?*

BOX #5: Exceptions

I certainly can't say that change is always for the better;
but what I can say is that improvement necessitates change.
—G. Lichtenberg, *The Little Book of Consolation*

Nothing happens all the time.
—Michael Durrant

To someone experiencing a problem, the notion that it might vary or even disappear is occasionally almost beyond comprehension. A seminal discovery of the Mental Research Institute's work was that problems are often maintained by the *belief* that the problem is invariant, as the attempted solutions to a counselee's problem often maintain or exacerbate it. Like Durrant, we believe that nothing never changes; that is, *problems vary.* It is often the counselee's view that his or her problem *always happens.* Because she or he may not notice "difference(s) that make a difference" (Bateson 1979), these exceptions remain unseen or ignored. The helper's role is *to bring the differences to the foreground* so that they can be reexamined. Then, once the client begins to view differences, the helper's role is to *create significance* so that the exceptions become as important as (or more important than) the problem in the counseling.

This concept is vital to the CBC model, as exceptions are the building blocks of change, the focus of agency and meaning as clients move forward. Eve Lipchik (1988, 4) has defined exceptions in this way: Exceptions are those behaviors, perceptions, thoughts and feelings that contrast with the complaint and have the potential of leading to a solution if amplified by the therapist and/or increased by the client.

Most notable is the idea that exceptions are *already happening*. Rather than invent, predict, or suppose exceptions could happen, we believe that exceptions can be located in the current and recent past experience of the counselee. Any difference in timing, frequency, control, and so on that relates directly to the person's view and experience of the problem should be capitalized on. The reason: we hold that any current, relevant exceptions to a problem will fit better with the counselee's change process and have a greater chance of continuing. Although pastors may have personal and counseling illustrations of what *could* be useful, we have found that what *is* currently useful creates an atmosphere that virtually eliminates failure. After all, if one is already doing something to affect one's problem, one can do it again!

The key to making exceptions meaningful seems to be in the helper's attitude or stance, not in the exceptions themselves. If we are simply holding to the "power of positive thinking," then we are in danger of becoming Pollyanna. Also, if we believe that any exception is relevant, then we are in danger of trivializing the person's experience. Locating meaningful exceptions, both volitional and serendipitous, in the counselee's current and near-current experience takes cooperation between helper and client. Not all exceptions are created equal.

BOX #6: Questions that Highlight Pre-Session Change

Michele Weiner-Davis and her colleagues (1987) conducted research that focused on the following question: *"Many people experience changes around their problem between the time they call for the first appointment and the first session, often for the better. Have you experienced any positive changes since you first called?"* Their research revealed that nearly two-thirds of those beginning counseling indicated experiencing some relief or positive change in their situations *before they actually began the first session.*

Capitalizing on the *possibility* of difference is important in our model. Because engendering hope in the initial contacts is so important, the helper should focus on purposefully directing the client's attention toward this possibility. Along with the time-honored methods of active listening and empathetic joining, this technique allows for the recognition of difference and the creation of positive movement toward change from the first contact.

Pre-session change is sometimes evident but often overlooked or seen as irrelevant. Counselors tend to ignore this supposed "flight into health" and move to explore the "real" problems. Sometimes a couple will say that things went well for the first two years and then problems started. It is common for therapists to say, "Ah, that was the honeymoon period; then the *real* problems became evident." However, a CBC counselor could just as easily say, "Ah, that was the *real* strength of the relationship; then a few difficulties developed." It's a matter of perspective and emphasis.

We would suggest that you ask this question early in the first session, just as it is written above. After probing the possibility of change with the counselee, the following questions may be of help to you by illustrating the kinds of question that may elicit evidence of pre-session change:

- So things are a little bit better for you. How have you managed to cut down on your crying since you first called to make an appointment?
- What would your _____ (mom, dad, teacher) say about you now that you've cut down on your talking in class?
- So things are not exactly the same as when you called last week. What have you been doing the past week that brought this about? (Point out the possibility of the person's control of the change.)
- So you've noticed less anxiety in your life since you first called. How did you do this?
- How did you get the idea to get a "head start" on this?

BOX #7: Exceptions-Finding Questions: Enhancing Existing and Past Successes

If you heard someone ask, "Hey—still tearing up the links, you old warhorse?" you probably would assume that there is some truth behind the question. Most of us would infer that the person to whom the question is directed (at least) plays golf and (perhaps) plays well.

William Swann and his colleagues (Swann, Giuliano, and Wegner 1982) have conducted a large number of experiments involving inference in conversation around the topic of introversion/extroversion. They found that asking leading questions has remarkable effects. First, when hearing a leading question, observers tend to believe that "the recipient was the kind of person who 'deserved' the question" (p. 1032). Observers not involved in the conversation tend to believe that the questioner must have evidence or the question would not be asked. Second, asking leading questions may actually draw out behavioral evidence supporting the question. That is, if experience exists to support the premise, the question draws it out. Swann and his colleagues found that, even if the questioner drew questions randomly from a jar of both introversion and extroversion questions, he or she would find evidence to support it. Finally, respondents who are asked leading questions often change the way they view themselves because of the questions asked and the evidence they give to support the questions. The researchers' conclusion: "If people are repeatedly confronted with such questions, they may permanently change their self-conceptions" (p. 1034). Asking questions about positive change and competence elicits evidence, convinces everyone involved that this is the right direction to go, and significantly influences self-conceptions.

Others may believe in a "right" or "correct" way to resolve problems. When a counselor takes this view, then a great deal of counseling becomes dominated by the "coulds"—"I could do this" or "You could try this." We believe in taking the low road to change, holding to the idea that every problem pattern contains some sort of exception; our job is to find it and exploit it. We see an important part of what we do as identifying exceptions to problem-dominated perceptions and behaviors. This activity is closely tied to the foundational idea that small change leads to greater change. We also hold to the idea that it is easier to continue a behavior or belief than it is to start a new one. Locating exceptions within the counselee's experience is the first step toward maintaining existing positive change, and we *know* they are there!

Once we have located meaningful exceptions to the problem experience, we attempt to investigate the counselee's sense of agency around that exception. Simply put, we believe that the possibility of continuing change is enhanced when people believe they have a "say" in what happens. If the changes one experiences are attributed to outside influences only, then the counselee's sense of influence is minimized. By asking leading questions around the counselee's influence of the change process, she or he has the opportunity to examine, consider, and decide on his or her options to push forward and control the direction, rate, and sphere of the continuing change. Therefore, we always assume that the client has some element of control over the change that has taken place.

Here are some questions that can guide counseling toward exceptions:

- When is it less frequent (intense, severe)?
- Who else noticed that you changed? In what way could you tell that he or she noticed?
- When is it different in any way? How did you figure out that doing _____ helps?
- There are times, I am sure, when you would expect the problem to happen, but it doesn't. How do you get that to happen?
- What is different when the problem could have gotten the best of you, but you did something to prevent it? What did you do?

Creating Exceptions: Separating the person from the problem

Externalizing (White 1989) is one way of affecting a problem definition and the experience of a problem's influence. White found that many of his counselees had difficulty separating experience and identity. For example, a little boy with bladder control difficulties did not just have a problem with enuresis—he was an "enuretic," a "bed wetter," or a "naughty boy." These descriptions were given him by helpers, parents, professionals, and the boy himself, and it was constantly reinforced through the use of such terms. One way that White discovered to separate the problem from the person was to "externalize" it. That is, White would ask questions that presupposed that the person was NOT identical with the problem, asking questions that would allow for new descriptions to evolve that separated the problem from the person. "In this process, the problem becomes a separate entity and thus external to the person who was, or the relationship that was, ascribed the problem" (p. 5).

Objectifying a problem as something outside of the person often allows for opposition to the problem without opposing the person, and alliances—in the helper/counselee relationship and in outside relationships—can be formed to contest the problem. Once again, this is a method for talking about the influence of a problem in a different way, one that is nonpejorative and different enough to allow for change. Some examples:

- How has what happened to you held you back?
- Are there ways you have been able not to allow your feelings of _____ to cripple you?
- Were there ways that the problem tried to stop you from talking about it?
- When the _____ takes over, what is your life like?

Creating Exceptions: Understanding the impact of the problem

Another prominent, related way of moving toward solving problems involves what White (1989) has called "relative influence questioning." This process "encourages persons to map the influence of the problem in their lives and relationships . . . [and] encourages persons to map their own influence in the 'life' of the problem" (p. 8). This line of questioning allows the person to describe freely the effects of the problem in many areas of his or her life, how it affects relationships as well as personal experiences. By mapping the problem's influence, the helper will be exposed to numerous realms of possibility for exceptions as the counselee describes the various paths, times, and manifestations of the problem.

For example, when Bob came to the office complaining of "depression" (again, remembering that the counselee's description is temporary and experiential, not determined or established), he was encouraged to talk about how "the depression" had influenced his life, both positively and negatively.

FNT: OK, so it's depression. What is depression like, for you?
Bob: It's like a hole.
FNT: OK.
B: Yeah, like this dark place.
FNT: How does it affect you?
B: Well . . . when I'm depressed like this, I'm all sad, and I avoid people.
FNT: What else does it do?
B: Just sort of overall hopeless.
FNT: Does it ever have a positive side?
B: No. Well, I do get to sleep in a lot! (*laughs*)

FNT: (*laughs*) Yeah, some of us would like to do that more! Anything
       else that depression does to you?
B: No, not that I can think of.

   At this point, the helper shifts to a mapping of the counselee's influence over the problem. "These questions bring forth information that
contradicts the problem-saturated description of . . . life, and assists
persons to identify their competence and resourcefulness in the face of
adversity" (White, 1989, pp. 9–10). As you can see in the example
above, Bob allowed talk about "the depression" in a way that was
external to him, even though he did not externalize it himself. In the
following continuation of the same session, you can see how Bob
responds to questions about his influence over "the depression," bringing out experiences he had previously overlooked.

FNT: OK . . . so, let's talk a bit about something else that's important,
       at least for me. Tell me about a recent time when the depression
       didn't have such a powerful grip on you.
B: (*startled*) Excuse me?
FNT: Well, most people are affected by depression in a variety of ways.
       Since you're a unique person—right?
B: I guess so. (*laughs*)
FNT: —I would assume your encounters with depression—you know,
       when it takes over—are unique to you!
B: OK. (*knits his brow*). So you want to know when it's . . .
FNT: Different.
B: Different. OK. Well, sometimes it's worse than other times. I
       mean, like Tuesday, it wasn't as bad.
FNT: How did you resist it?
B: Well, I got out of bed—I had a meeting that I just couldn't miss,
       you know, one for my house loan—I'm refinancing it, and
       Wendy (*his wife*) was meeting me there, and . . . well, it pretty
       much stayed away all day, as a matter of fact.
FNT: How did you do that?
B: Do what?
FNT: Push it away, not let it take over?
B: I just had things to do. It just stayed away.
FNT: So, what other times did you push it away?
B: Sometimes it doesn't work for a long time, but . . . when I'm
       having fun, it isn't so bad.

FNT: So, if you're having fun, you can keep it pushed aside.
B: Yeah, for about as long as the fun lasts . . . or as long as I make the fun last!
FNT: OK, great! When else?

Bob continues to identify exceptions to the problem-saturated viewpoint he brought with him to this session. These exceptions must be significant to Bob in order to provide new ways of relating to "the depression"; therefore, not all exceptions are created equal! Most counselees will have the experience of relating several (or many) exceptions to their usual problem-dominated ordeal, and a few will make more sense than others to both the helper and the counselee. The most relevant exception experiences should become the focus of continuation tasks (keeping the changes going), increased influence tasks (taking the offensive on the problem more frequently, in new settings, etc.), and noticing tasks (paying attention to additional moments of influence over the problem during the time between sessions). (These are described below when we talk about how to keep change going.)

Some people work on naming the problem, to create a visualization of the problem as residing outside the person yet inside the person's sphere of influence. White's (1989) examples are cute and effective— encopresis becomes "Sneaky Poo," while enuresis is renamed "Sneaky Wee." Many children respond to drawing pictures of their "nightmare monster," and the externalization of sexual abuse memories via drawings has been a powerful tool for both children and adults. It is important to remember that externalization is not the removal of responsibility for change; it is simply creating distance, the separation of the person from the problem, so it can be addressed in a different way as one searches for exceptions, agency, and difference.

The following questions may be helpful to guide your thinking around relative influence questioning. Keep in mind that this is a question-driven model—only the counselee can supply viable exceptions, and you will be very surprised at their unique examples of agency!

Creating Exceptions: Mapping the influence of the problem
• How has the problem been a problem in your life?
• In what way has this problem had an effect on you/your life?
• In what way(s) is the problem still affecting you?
• In what way(s) has this problem kept you from moving forward in a way you would like?

- How would your _____ (father, girlfriend, etc.) say this problem has had an effect on your life? Would you agree?

Creating Exceptions: Mapping the influence of the person on the problem
- When have you been able to affect the _____ (timing, length of stay, intensity) of the depression?
- Most people report times when they are able to beat this fatigue factor. When was the last time you were able to keep it at bay, even if it was just for an hour or so?
- (For nightmares:) Tell me about the last time you fought off this monster. Did you do it yourself, or did your mom (dad, sister, and so on) help you do this?
- (For bedwetting:) I'll bet there was a time, and probably not too long ago, when you outran Sneaky Wee and made it to the toilet. Let's put on our thinking caps—was it in the past week, or maybe even in the past couple of nights?
- (For couples:) Tell me when this "lack of trust" didn't come between the two of you—how did you do it?

BOX #8: Interpreting the Exceptions:
Making Exceptions Meaningful

This line of inquiry looks into two specific areas: personal agency and self-perception. It is our assumption that every client and counseling pastor makes sense out of exceptions; that is, we all decide "why" something happens as an anomaly to the rule. We believe it is vital to promote explanations that increase choice and to ask questions that are slanted toward understandings that increase the person's sense of agency and promote self-understandings based on strength and resilience. Whenever an exception to the problem is generated, we ask questions like the following to elevate competency and positive ownership:
- How do you account for your ability to do this?
- Is this something that surprised you about yourself . . . the fact that you were able to stand up to the problem in this way?
- What about you helped you to be able to do this?
- Did you know before you did _____ that you would be able to do it? How did you know that about yourself?
- What was different about this situation compared with one when the problem was more in charge? What was different about you?

- What would your (friend, mother, etc.) say if I were to ask how they think you did this?
- Did this escape from the problem come easily to you, or was it something you found difficult?
  - *If response is "easy"*: How do you account for your ability to make something other people find very difficult seem easy?
  - *If response is "difficult"*: How do you account for your ability to do something like this even though it was hard to do?

BOX #9: Keeping Change Going

We have almost arrived at Cucamonga! Earlier in this chapter, we began using this competency-based "map" by discussing socializing, moving on to goal setting, and transversing exceptions. In keeping with the assumptions of our map, we now move toward the conclusion of the session by focusing on the theme of change. Many models of counseling emphasize tasks or homework in order to provide structure between sessions, create paradoxical interactions, attain a new skill, and so on. Within our model of counseling, the goal is to maintain changes that have already been identified. Although this may not seem as profound as paradoxical injunctions, skill attainment, or baseline determination, it is essential to this model because it provides avenues for practice, discovery, and success.

We have identified three types of tasks which we have successfully incorporated into our model of model. First, *noticing tasks* (see de Shazer et al. 1986) create an expectation of success and can be used with nearly every presenting problem, family type, or individual. One simply asks the counselee something like this: "In the time between sessions, I would like for you to notice times when things are better (different, improving, etc.) and come back ready to talk about these times. It would help us make faster progress if you could be as specific as possible."

This is a valuable intervention for several reasons. Giving a noticing task is congruent with what you have been attempting to do during the session, as it is a continued focus on the counselee's competence. As we have said, people who are stuck tend to notice, or focus on, examples of the problem or of failure and tend not to notice those successes (however small) that are actually happening. This task reorients them to be on the lookout for differences.

Next, embedded in the task is the assumption that what you have identified as strengths, exceptions, and so on will be present in the client's life during the next week or two. Also, this task is ripe with success. Even if the counselee fails to pay close attention to exceptions as they happen, it is a terrific place to begin the next session as it allows for a review of the week based on success and positive change instead of continuous reviews of the problem's influence.

Second, one could continue the session's trend by assigning *continuation tasks*. Although one might appear Forrest Gumpish, these are simply stated, simply understood, and simply attained in the life of most counselees. The helper should take the time at the end of the session to review the successes, exceptions, and counselee influences with the counselee. Together, you talk about continuing exceptions that are within the influence of the counselee, defining them in such a way that the counselee cannot lose. For example:

FNT: It seems as though you have a great deal of influence over
            your depression. Would you agree with this?
Counselee: Yes, it seems like it. I mean, we listed so many ways I have.
FNT: Well, for the next week, I would like for you to simply con-
            tinue what you're doing without making any major
            changes. If what you're doing works, you certainly should
            be able to continue it!
C: No problem—I just do what I've been doing?
FNT: Right.

The MRI model (Watzlawick, Weakland, and Fisch 1974) of restraining change has been a powerful intervention for decades. Many counselees find change to be difficult, partly because their attempts to change inhibit the very thing they seek. By being directed to "go slow" (*sic*) and bridle change, the counselee is relieved of the pressure to change, and change is simply allowed to happen.

Third, one may assign *increased influence tasks*. If the counselee has identified moments of success over the problem and believes that he or she has some influence in this success, a congruent task would be to increase this influence in a *small*, specific way, framing this as an experiment. Once again, this should be given so that the chance of success is great. The following example may help:

Most people find this difficult, but . . . between now and the next time we meet, I would like you to take a small step in the direction we've identified today to increase your happiness from a ____ (counselee's number) to a ____ (add one to the counselee's estimation).

As stated earlier, since "most people find this difficult," failure can be avoided by appealing to this idea if the counselee does not move up the scale. If the counselee succeeds, then time can be spent on what makes him or her unique, since "most people find this difficult."

Throughout this chapter, we have attempted to provide you with the most useful ideas we have for beginning your journey into PossibilityLand. Perhaps a more useful map could be created for another approach to counseling; however, we believe that consistency with one's assumptions—both theoretical and pragmatic—is the best way to proceed in pastoral counseling. In the following chapters, we provide case examples which will illuminate our use of the competency-based counseling map as well as additional areas of pastoral and lay application. If you get lost, reorient, check the map key and travel instructions, and strike out for your goal again. Improving one's pastoral counseling is the same as getting to Carnegie Hall—the only path is practice, practice, practice!

5

TWO CASE EXAMPLES OF COMPETENCY-BASED COUNSELING

Many books we have read fail to illustrate concepts, perceptions, and interventions for the reader. This chapter presents two case examples illustrating how we apply our pastoral counseling model. No approach is perfect, and we have case failures as well as successes. The following cases are fairly typical, however, and relate directly to pastoral counseling settings, contexts, issues, and presenting problems. We hope you find them illuminating and useful.

CASE #1:
"WHEN PAST CHRISTIAN COUNSELING FAILS"

You met Maggie in our introductory chapter. A woman about fifty years of age, she sought counseling and came to the first session alone. I (FNT) had been recommended by Maggie's counselor when she learned that she was moving to my vicinity.

Maggie had been married twenty years to Les, and they had one child, a sixteen-year-old girl named Shelly. Maggie placed a great value on counseling. She had sought out pastoral guidance from time to time throughout her adult life. Also, Maggie had continually been in formal counseling with two different helpers over the past two years, seeking help for herself and her family. Her husband, Les, reportedly suffered from bouts of depression that kept him from participating in family life for days at a time. Their daughter, Shelly, was a high school senior who struggled with rules both at school and at home.

Maggie's primary concern focused on her desire for "Christian counseling." She reported that all of her past helpers had approached their problems with what she called "biblically-based principles," and she wanted counseling to address her faith as well as her family and personal needs. Her last counselor, with whom she and/or her family had met weekly for two years, told Maggie that I would certainly hold to the same values as she.

Session One

Maggie came alone to this session (and the rest of our meetings as well). She was breathing hard when she appeared in my outer office, a result of getting lost "in this big city." As it turned out, this was Maggie's first venture out of the home since moving to Fort Worth nearly a month before.

Maggie: I'm sorry I'm late. I had no idea your office was so far away!
FNT: That's quite all right. I had no place else to be. Besides, you're only a few minutes late. Catch your breath!
M: You see *(takes two deep breaths)*, I've never driven in a city this big. I really hate heavy traffic, it scares me to death.
FNT: Well, then, you're to be congratulated for coming. You must have a good reason for coming today.

Here we settled into a brief discussion about her family members, the move to Fort Worth, and her past counseling experiences.

FNT: So, what's most important for me to know as we get started?
M: Well, mostly, I'm here for me. But it's my daughter who has the problems. You see, she has, um, an addictive personality disorder and—
FNT: What is that, and how is that a problem?
M: Well, right now she's a senior in high school, and she has been acting out sexually. I know she has been drinking and maybe using drugs.
FNT: What drugs do you suspect she's used?
M: Pot, probably; I don't know.
FNT: OK. And how does this affect you and your family?
M: Well, I learned in counseling (with past helper) that I'm the one who's really responsible for my family. I take it all on, you know.
FNT: You mean, it's your responsibility to make everything work? Or is it that you feel responsible?
M: Both. Yes. *(laughs)* I mean, I know I can't make it perfect, but that doesn't stop me from trying! *(laughs)*.
FNT: So . . . how're you doing, at making it all perfect?
M: So far, I guess I'd have to say I'm failing pretty miserably.

Here, Maggie began to cry openly, talking about her continued failures with her daughter and in her marriage. The conversation moved to comforting her in her pain and validating her experience (Cade and O'Hanlon 1993, Durrant 1995). After a few minutes, I decided to take a tack toward solution talk.

FNT: OK, so . . . what's the most important thing we can tackle today, while you're here?

M: I guess . . . *(pause)* . . . it would have to be getting control of my daughter. If that happened, our lives would be so much better.

FNT: Tell me something: is anything different with your daughter since you moved here?

M: Actually, I don't know . . . *(pause)* . . . all of the trouble we had with her was in (previous home city).

FNT: You mean, she hasn't been in trouble since you moved here?

M: Well, no . . . but I'm sure she's doing the same things.

FNT: What have you noticed that is better, regarding your daughter? I mean, since you moved here?

M: Well, she seems happy with her new friends.

FNT: How do you know that?

M: Well, she tells me she likes school, and that means she likes her friends. She's on the golf team, but I don't think she'll keep it up—

FNT: How do you think she's managed to make friends so quickly here?

M: Oh, she's really a likable kid. She never has problems making friends. In fact, we usually never are alone—she has friends over all the time. It's hard to get any time without other kids around—

FNT: So, how did you manage to make your home open to her new friends? I mean, you just moved here, and all the hustle and bustle that goes with that—it could be disruptive . . .

M: Oh, I love having them around—I feel like that's something I can do for her, to make our home open for her . . . and then, that way I get to know who she's with, you know?

The conversation focused here on how happy her daughter seemed to be since moving to the new city and school. My focus was on

Maggie's success in being different, on not trying so hard to make things work. We continued:

FNT: What do you think this move could mean to Shelly? I mean, she's been here a month and she hasn't been kicked out of school or gotten drunk.

M: I don't know. Maybe she can turn a new leaf—I mean, turn over a new leaf . . .

FNT: Maybe she already has, to some extent, from what you've said.

M: Maybe.

FNT: What have you been doing differently?

M: I don't understand.

FNT: I mean, what have you been doing to make things work?

M: Well, I know what I've *not* been doing—I've been staying out of Shelly's life—

FNT: Really? Has that worked for you?

M: So far. I mean, I don't know if I can if she gets in trouble—

FNT: How are you making a life for yourself here?

Here we discussed the various neighborhood groups, church meetings, and school functions that Maggie had already attended. She felt that her contact with new people was easy for her, and she knew that getting isolated always made things worse. Also, we made the connection between Maggie's giving up trying so hard and Shelly's doing OK on her own. The session ended on a positive note:

FNT: So . . . how about you paying attention this week to times when you let Shelly handle things, and also notice when things are going well for Shelly. Sound OK?

M: Sure.

Session Two

Two weeks passed between the first two sessions. In this second session, Maggie related seeing significant changes in her life and in her relationship with Shelly. She related several incidents in which she allowed Shelly to "have her own life" (make her own decisions), and she reported that Shelly was continuing to "stay out of trouble." In fact, Shelly was thriving in school, and Maggie could not remember one incident of family or school trouble.

Maggie was noticing a significant difference in one particular area of her own life: when she took care of herself and did not take care of all the needs of her husband and daughter, her quality of life improved.

We agreed to wait one month before meeting, to see how this new "pattern of responsibility" would adjust in Maggie's life. She agreed to "stay out of things" in Shelly's life whenever possible by taking care of herself. This relates directly to de Shazer's (1991) idea that, if something isn't working, one must do something different to get different results.

Session Three

Maggie began this session by relating a mishap that occurred on her way home from our last session. While driving on the freeway, Maggie's car had inexplicably stalled, and she guided the car to the side of the road. She related the terror she felt, being alone on a strange highway at dusk, but she struck out for the next exit on foot instead of waiting in her car and hoping for someone to stop and assist her. While she walked, a telephone repairman stopped and loaned her his cellular phone on which to call her husband.

Instead of viewing this as a setback, Maggie related that, in spite of her terror, she felt competent to handle her misfortune. She said:

M: You know, in the past, I would've gone home and locked myself in the house for a month if something like this had happened!

FNT: Well, how did you manage to resist that temptation?

M: I guess I just knew that I could handle it. The weeks before (the incident) had given me time to think and to pray, pray that God would show me some better way of handling things. Well, He did, and it's so simple! Why didn't I see it before?

FNT: See what?

M: That I needed to let go and let God. I needed to let go and let Shelly and Les and the whole world work out things without my meddling.

FNT: Well, I'm wondering how you let yourself let go? I mean, that is not something most people can do.

M: Well, you know, this past week was really a test for me. Shelly has been out of control. She's been kicked out of a class at school, and she got into a fight with another girl—I mean, pulling hair and everything! You know, my first thought was, "I need to get up to that school and give that principal a piece of my mind," you know, try to work out things for her by standing up for her. Well, I didn't! I stayed out of it, and she worked it out. She even tried to quit the golf team, but I wouldn't sign it (the form to change classes, dropping golf and adding a study hall). I told her, "You just work it out." She cussed me, and she stomped around, and she threw a real tantrum, but I stuck to my guns.

FNT: Well . . . I'm in suspense. What happened?!

M: She worked it out, somehow—I don't even know how. All I know is, I'm doing wonderfully . . .

Maggie went on to describe how she had difficulties with her own mother and father over money and family matters during the time between our sessions, and how she had "drawn her boundaries" and not attempted to smooth everything over for them. Les had also been "depressed" to the point that he had holed up with his computer every night after work for several days. However, instead of her usual attempts to coax him into interacting with her (and failing), she "let him be" and continued with her now-normal routine of church activities and handicraft hobbies.

Near the end of this session, Maggie stated that she felt she would like to "take a break from counseling." She felt she was handling things well herself and that life was going to go on with some "bumps" no matter how much counseling she got. When I asked about how she would continue to deal with her daughter's problems, she said, "I can't keep taking responsibility for the whole world." She had faith that Shelly would find some way to work out her own problems, and that God would "do the worrying for her."

Follow Up

Approximately one month after this session, which was our last time together, Maggie called to ask for a legal referral. The police from the city in which they used to live had contacted Maggie, asking to question Shelly about a crime Shelly might have witnessed. After referring her to a competent local attorney for this immediate problem, I asked how things had been going for her and her family. She said that she was still doing "wonderfully," in spite of some rough moments in the family. She was maintaining her personal strategy to "stay out of other people's business" and it was working well for her.

I usually do telephone follow-up with former counselees six and twelve months after counseling ends. Maggie did this for me after about a year in two ways. First (as related in the Introduction), Maggie called me on behalf of a friend for a referral, and she reported that, in spite of some moments of difficulty, she was doing well. Also, I received a Christmas card from her about the same time. Her cheery note read: "Thank you for your support and for being there when I need[ed it]. Les said he wants to try to battle this 'blue feeling' [what she used to call depression] on his own . . . will keep you posted. We're doing great— because I'm doing great! All the best in the New Year. Maggie."

CASE #2: "A QUESTION OF OBEDIENCE"

Cynthia, age forty-four, called the church requesting a counseling appointment. She stated that she had remarried last year and was having difficulty with her new spouse, Jerry, and his children, Mark (age fourteen) and Lela (age twelve). Cynthia explained that she also had one daughter, Tammi (age fifteen), from her previous marriage to Steve who had passed away roughly five years ago after a long and difficult struggle with leukemia. In addition, she stated that she had been in counseling with a pastor at another church with no visible results so she "just quit going." She insisted on coming in on her own the first time because she knew that her husband "would argue with her about her going to counseling again." Below is an excerpt from the first and only interview for which she arrived approximately fifteen minutes after her scheduled appointment time.

It is important to note that with a competency-based approach to working with people, such things as late arrivals are not interpreted as passive-aggressive, manipulative, resistant, or controlling behaviors. This stance is a by-product of the more general assumption that seeks to abstain from activities geared toward forming causal explanations about those with whom we work.

Cynthia: I'm sorry I'm late. I guess time just got away from me.

JC: That's no problem, Cynthia, but since we've only got till ten before the hour . . . if you like let's start by—

C: Well . . . I'm sorry, I don't mean to interrupt . . . but there was one thing I was wondering about on the way over here.

JC: Please, fire away.

C: Now don't get me wrong, because I know Jerry would never come to counseling, and I would do this for me at this point, but—I don't understand what good it's going to do with just me coming in. I mean . . . well . . . if you're going to do marital counseling don't you have to have two people?

JC: I suspect that a lot of people have that impression, but my experience has been that a lot of the time it doesn't make much difference. As a matter of fact, now that I stop and think about it, sometimes it makes matters worse, you know . . . say if a spouse is forced to show up and they sit there scowling the whole time. I can tell you that definitely doesn't work! Funny . . . I seem to remember someone once saying that "a part" *(spelled out loud)* is not really "apart."

C: Hmm . . . OK.

The beginning of the above conversation highlights a notion in competency work of wholism. This is a systemic idea which states that a change in one relational aspect of a system will exert an effect upon other relational aspects within its larger system. Since it is assumed that one member of a family is capable of generating a "rippling effect" throughout the larger family system, we view the involvement of one earnest family member just as viable as engaging partners or an entire family.

JC: So, with that out of the way, what brings you in today?

C: I really can't live this way any more. *(Begins to get tearful)*
      (Pause)

JC: Would you be OK with telling me more about what that means?

C: *(Sniffling)* I'm all right . . . I didn't mean to come apart . . . it's just getting to be too much. It was this week five years ago that my first husband passed away . . .

JC: I'm very sorry.

C: . . . and if it's not the children always squabbling at one another over the least little thing it's Jerry coming home and giving me the silent treatment for reasons I don't understand. On top of that, what really gets to me is that he sits and teaches in the adult

Sunday school and acts like this spiritual hotshot. He's the biggest hypocrite!

JC: Whew, it sounds like there's a lot going on.

C: *(Silence)*

JC: O.K . . . .I try to keep things simple and if I heard you right there are a bunch of things going on. So I was just wondering if we could come up with somewhere to start with all this. Like, if we could rate all of these things in order of their importance, which one might you like to put at the top of the list?

The counselee, in reciting her litany of concerns, has offered multiple areas that are potential starting points. With this approach we honor what the counselee decides is the most important issue worthy of our mutual attention.

C: *(Pause)* My marriage to Jerry. From the start things used to go pretty well between us and it seems like out of the blue about six months ago things began getting worse. I try to do things but he just doesn't notice or seem to care.

JC: So if I'm hearing you right, a possible goal in your coming here would be to have a better relationship with Jerry?

C: Yes.

JC: You mentioned that the relationship used to go pretty well at the beginning, so I'm curious, what do you think was the reason for that?

C: I really have no idea. I've thought about that and all I can come up with is that it was new at the time.

JC: OK. In light of that, what do you think is important for me to know at this point?

C: It's this silent treatment stuff . . . in the bedroom when he changes, at the dinner table, in the car, everywhere. His dad does the same thing to his mother. Last time we were over for the usual after church lunch his dad didn't say a word to Harriet or me. We never talk anymore.

JC: When you say silent treatment, how does he actually indicate to you that he doesn't wish to talk?

C: Well . . . that's hard to say. It's a look or a feeling I get from him. Tell you what though, sometimes I think he's paying me back for disagreeing with him. He says all the time that when I disagree with how he wants to handle things, say, with the kids, that I'm being disobedient.

JC: OK. I've got an idea. If you could scale your relationship from, say, 0 being the pits and 10 would be about as good as it gets, where would you place your relationship today?

C: 0 to 10, eh? I would put it—oh, I don't know—say a 4 or a 5.

JC: OK. So if we average that we'd have a 4.5?

C: Yeah, I guess you could say that.

JC: If Jerry were here, what might you guess he'd say?

C: Oh, I don't know . . . probably about the same.

JC: OK. So when, let's say, you guys are at a 5.5 what do you think will be different about the relationship?

C: Uhm . . . well, you know . . . we would be happier and there'd be more communication.

JC: Well, there's communication in the relationship now. It just doesn't sound like very useful communication.

C: Right . . .

JC: So what would be happening in the relationship instead of the silent treatment and that other stuff?

C: You mean specifically? Well, maybe we'd talk more to each other . . . no, not just talking . . . he . . . no, we could talk about things that we disagree on and not end up fighting. Then I wouldn't have a reason to be disobedient!

Cynthia continued to talk at length about the difficulty and frustration of getting her viewpoints across, of how she was losing the desire to make Jerry happy, and how when she was "disobedient" Jerry would punish her for days with the silent treatment. She further related that during her first husband's illness she had been silent through the entire process. She conveyed the sense that no one, from the doctors to insurance representatives, appeared to value her input when her husband became acutely ill, and she wasn't going to let that happen ever again. Because it would easy to get stuck in ambiguous or accusatory language, a scaling question such as the one above offered a pragmatic way of assessing the relationship in more concrete terms. In addition, it expanded the options for talking about the relationship in terms of "instead of" as opposed to the "absence of" something. Note that there was a conscious effort to talk about the "relationship" instead of two or multiple individuals' viewpoints at this point in the conversation.

JC: You know, I was just wondering, with all this talk about disobedience, if it could it be an opinion problem rather than an obedience problem or maybe even an entirely different kind of problem?

C: Well . . . possibly an opinion, sure, but he thinks that he's always right. You know what its like . . . this is my position and because I'm the husband that means my ideas count the most. And to make matters worse, he's an engineer, so he says that he's always thinking things through logically. He is always complaining that I bug him too much about feelings. What I don't understand is that it wasn't always this way. *(Pause)* I mean we could talk about closeness and things like that. I used to be able to make him happy.

JC: Are you afraid that you are losing some sense of your ability to make your husband happy?

C: I don't know what you mean by that.

JC: Sorry, bad question. When was there a time in the past that you felt you contributed to your husband's happiness when he was, say, really down in the dumps?

C: Sure. There was a time when we were first married that his supervisor at work was finding fault with Jerry's work for no good reason. He would come home upset and gloomy. I didn't ask him what was going on, but I could see it in his face. So I pretended not to be concerned and just went on and fixed dinner.

JC: How were you able to do that?

C: I just decided not to let the evening be ruined, and if he's not going to do anything about it then I will. I learned a long time ago when Steve was very sick not to collapse on the outside just because of what was going on inside me.

JC: That's sounds terribly difficult. If you don't mind me asking what did that experience tell you about you?

C: I learned that I could be strong and be there for my children and myself. It was horrible . . . all the chemo, the sickness, and the hurt.

JC: You know, during such a devastating illness experience did it come to you that you had this marvelous gift—I mean to see what's going on and things being terribly difficult—am I getting this right?—you can just decide to pull yourself up and be strong for yourself and your children?

C: Yeah, I suppose . . . but it wasn't as easy as it sounds.

JC: No, you're right. I'm sorry; these types of things don't come easy. So, I'm curious: what was different when you were able to do that for Jerry?

C: We talked a little on the couch and there wasn't this cloud hanging over everybody's head and everything was good enough. You know, just enjoyed being there.

JC: You were enjoying the relationship?

C: Oh, yeah. The kids were either gone or upstairs doing something. And Jerry and I could just talk and there wasn't any pressure.

JC: So when the relationship is going well—I want to make sure I got this—you and your husband are more relaxed or something?

C: Sure, when the pressure's off it's easier on everybody.

JC: I was just wondering about something. When your husband gets home are you usually there?

C: Yes, most of the time anyway.

JC: I was just playing with the idea of what might be different if you were to try this "pressure's off" expression and observe through the rest of the week what happens. I mean, who knows, instead of the silent treatment—

C: Sounds reasonable to me.

JC: What do you think might be an obstacle to keep you from trying this experiment?

C: Well, it's easier to put that expression on when I'm in a good mood. If the kids haven't been nagging and going after one another it's a piece of cake.

JC: Good, I'm glad you brought that up. If our goal is to see what's different about the relationship, can we come up something that might ensure that the kids don't fight?

C: That's probably not possible. But this arguing and silent treatment is killing me so I'll just try to stay in a good mood with the kids too.

JC: Great! Before we go too much further I had a funny thought. I was wondering what your life would look like if in the near future it was going the way you wanted it to between you and Jerry.

C: Hmm . . . I think we would talk more about things and not get into it every time I don't always agree with Jerry's opinion. We disagree a lot about how to raise the kids . . . I mean, teenagers are hard enough without the hassles of arguing about them.

JC: OK. So you would be talking about things that maybe you had different opinions on and not fight?

C: Yeah, and he would quit this "I'm the teacher" thing.

JC: Sure, but talking about that might lead to trouble. What at this point do you think Jerry might have to say about the relationship if it were to get back on track?

C: That's hard . . . I think he would say just about the same thing, you know, arguing over the children and not just one more thing to add to the misery right now.

JC: I'm curious. Is there something that you could teach Jerry about you in a way that wouldn't come across as teachy?

C: You mean . . . like something I've learned?

JC: Could be, could be anything like that. I was thinking about your gift for making it through extremely difficult situations with a strong heart and your integrity intact.

C: I'll have to think on that.

JC: Sure. Sorry . . . something like that would probably take some time and planning. Well, getting back to the safe talk, are there safe topics in the relationship that can be discussed right now that don't provoke or make things worse?

C: I don't know if it is the topics or that certain days are worse for him than others. Until now I never really gave it much thought. I know there are times when we manage well enough but now it is not as clear as when I got here. I mean, if he has learned this from his dad . . . it makes sense you know, because that was something that took over forty years for him to get. Maybe it's not all just Jerry.

JC: Well, sure, that's certainly a possibility. For all we know the silent treatment may have started out as doing something good for Jerry, like not blowing up and losing his temper, or something like that. Anyway, if I heard you right it sounds like this "pressure's off" expression might be worth experimenting with so you could notice what is different. It would be important to notice how the relationship does on certain days—I mean, maybe look for hints that silences might be an invitation to do something else. If you think there's an opening maybe tell him that you are willing to talk anytime he likes and just drop it from there. Does this seem to be a realistic first step with the goal of improving your relationship with Jerry?

C: I don't know . . . this seems too simple.

JC: Yes, Cynthia, but perhaps the simpler the better.

A phone call follow-up two weeks later found Cynthia and Jerry doing better. Cynthia reported success with the "pressure's off" expression and improvement with their relationship in addition to, oddly enough (her words), having spent the first week in a long time not arguing with the kids. She reported that the observation experiment was going well and that she was beginning to get a better sense of how to approach Jerry without the children present when there was something she wanted to discuss with him. Surprisingly, she admitted that she and Jerry had gotten away for the weekend for an anniversary celebration they had missed earlier!

COMMENTARY

First, not all our cases are brief. As Cade and O'Hanlon (1993, 5) have said, brief counseling means being "concerned with how to intervene as briefly and as economically as possible." It does not focus on the number of sessions (or minutes!). Instead, we simply find that taking a competency approach results in effective *and* efficient outcomes. Having a goal orientation and focusing on what is changeable generally makes for short-term contact with people presenting for pastoral counseling.

Second, these clients are not "typical." We believe in the following statements at the same time: (1) People are more alike than different (Whitaker 1990); and (2) Every person is a crosscultural experience. (O'Hanlon 1992).

These may seem contradictory, but we believe they are not. Taking each counselee, couple, or family seriously means that we cannot categorize them as "just like." Our approach focuses on the counselee's experience of the problem, no matter what the identifying category (de Shazer 1991). At the same time, we know that most people respond to curiosity, respect, and warm regard. Therefore, we concentrate on the counselee's idiosyncratic experience while, at the same time, maintaining a posture of inquisitiveness, honoring the counselee in time-honored ways, and taking cues from him or her to maintain a respectful position.

Finally, our primary goal in presenting these cases is to illustrate, not defend, our model. Every reader reads these transcriptions from a perspective that can find other ideas, problems, issues, and faults. We do not claim to have achieved perfection with these two cases. To paraphrase Karl Tomm (1991), we seek clarity, not certainty.

6

RESOURCE FOCUS
It's Not Just for
Counseling Anymore!

We have found that taking a solution orientation to life—and not only to counseling—has been tremendously rewarding. Whether we are counseling, teaching, or supervising in professional settings, we desperately seek solutions within the individuals and groups we encounter. But in addition to our professional applications, we have also created outlets for competency in church, social, school, business, and neighborhood settings. In this chapter, we would like to introduce a few ministry applications of the competency-based approach outside of formal pastoral counseling settings. Premarital interviewing, cell ministry, staff relations, and family wellness are touched by our approach in ways that may stimulate you in your personal ministry. It may prove transformational!

PREMARITAL INTERVIEWS:
THE BEGINNING OF THE JOURNEY

I suppose this is one of the great qualities of a pastoral counselor who,
in his belief that man is made in the image of God,
has this unconditional positive regard "built in." . . .
—Carl Whitaker (1989)

After several years of conducting premarital interviews using this approach, some tentative conclusions seem appropriate. First, couples are the experts on their own lives. Second, couples have gathered expectations and assumptions about their future family from previous experiences with their own family histories. Third, couples emerge from families with adaptive resources to meet life's demands. And fourth, couples are able to identify those aspects of premarital work that are useful both for their present and their future relationship.

97

These are certainly not earth-shattering admissions, but they are important for conducting competency-based premarital interviews.[1] Within a competency approach we acknowledge that there is no predetermined agenda for how to proceed other than to maintain our stance of respecting the couple's wishes, avoiding blame statements, and identifying strengths. Conducting competency-based premarital interviews using a genogram may provide the basis for a continued meaningful conversation that, in addition to clarifying expectations and illuminating assumptions, invites the couple to begin fully appreciating their own relational strengths and growth areas. In the words of McGoldrick and Gerson (1985), the use of the genogram can point the way to "new possibilities in the future" (p. 133).

"A genogram is a graphic representation of a multigenerational family constellation. Guerin and Pendagast (1976) call it 'a road map of the family relationship system' that shows names, ages, dates of marriages, divorces, deaths, illnesses, . . . key events, and other pertinent facts." (Simon, Stierlin, and Wynne 1985, 173). As a tool, a genogram can be used for many purposes, such as the identification of family secrets, myths, or loss. For our purposes, we use the genogram as a resource construction tool, identifying resiliency and positive stories in each person's family. Always keep von Foerster's dictum in mind: Believing is seeing! You can "find" or create anything in a genogram—we simply focus on aspects we believe are most useful within this pastoral counseling model.

This user-friendly approach involves recording family constituency and demographics, noteworthy events, characteristics and qualities of interaction among family members, and the process by which difficulties and resources are transacted through the generations of each partner's family. While we adhere to the redemptive and productive aspects of intergenerational relationships, we have noted that not all counselees believe that this is true for them. In addition, premarital interviews are often the first structured exposure couples have to verbalizing issues of guilt, trust, or remorse. As stated earlier, a competency approach does not exclude the less-than-positive or painful. Those wishing to work collaboratively with couples during the premarital process should stay respectful, flexible, and supportive, and "go where the couple goes." In the face of unpleasant facts, stories, or experiences, our practice is to impart a sense of validation and an appreciation for their difficulties with the hope of remaining open to family strengths, personal resources, and positive legacies (Thomas 1995a).

Once a basic understanding of genogram construction is established, we suggest that helpers create their own family genograms. This serves to facilitate a comfort level with the application of the genogram in interview settings. It also helps us examine the assumptions that we bring to the premarital setting (Thomas 1995a). If helpers adhere to the idea that particular aspects of family relationships, family history, and definitions of health and pathology are to be more highly valued than others, then an honest appraisal of these areas will serve to guide the helper.

We suggest that the first premarital interview be devoted to describing a genogram's component parts with the couple and to beginning the construction while the couple is present in the office. In conjunction with preparing the genogram, the helper may wish to make the couple aware of the benefits and potential difficulties associated with this approach, such as the "filling in the blanks" of information that is not close at hand. Our experience has been that, for many couples, the making of a family genogram is both surprising and informative when introduced in a collaborative manner. After the initial genogram is completed, we suggest that the couple take their respective diagrams and think about any facts, stories, or experiences that they think might be important to talk about the next time we meet. In addition, we follow Kuehl's (1995) lead and add that they should notice things that they believe are positive from each family and relationship to bring up at subsequent meetings.

For the remaining interviews, there are a few features that are important for helpers to keep in mind. The first might be called the "sphere of relative influence" questions (White and Epston 1990) which emphasize how the couple and their respective family members have dealt with certain issues such as substance abuse, anger, or divorce over time. These questions typically take forms such as, "What has been done in your family to contend successfully with this?"; "How do you think they managed to make things better?"; and "When were you able to respond differently to (the issue), and what did that tell you about yourself?" What is noteworthy with these types of questions is that most couples report a degree of influence in not succumbing to the problem. Moreover, in our counseling experience rarely has any given issue been able to gain absolute influence over every member of a family system, so couples are encouraged to notice the exceptions and reconnect with members of their extended families who could be supportive of them (Kuehl 1995).

Lest it go unsaid, "sphere of influence" questions are as applicable when inquiring about strengths and resources as they are for problem resolution. For example, a couple may be asked, "What legacies of hope and strength do you believe you have received from your family, and how might you bring the positive effects of that to your present relationship?"

Another series of questions involves what has been termed "back to the future generation" questions (Kuehl 1995). These are designed to help couples conceptualize in a clear, concise manner the changes they would like to have happen. A sample of questions: "Given the way it was in your family and the way you would like this relationship to be, what do you expect to be different for each of you in the future?" and "How are you going to know when you are on track with these changes?"

The third set of questions could be thought of as "collapsing inter-generational time" questions (Kuehl 1995). These questions are designed to evaluate whether particular problems have worsened or improved over the span of generations. Emphasizing the amount of progress, no matter how small, invites couples to experience a renewed sense of pride and accomplishment. Some example questions: "How are you already dealing with this issue more usefully than your mother or father did?" "What does this tell you about yourself and each other? As you stay on track with these changes, what do you suppose will be different (a week, a month, a year) from now?"

Before continuing further, let's take a look at the actual construction of a couple's genogram. We find that turning a legal size pad of plain paper lengthwise is ample room for recording the couple's two- or three- generational outline. After an appropriate conversation of "getting to know you," we prefer to proceed to an introduction of what a genogram represents and a description of how it may be used to facilitate this and the following premarital interviews.

Beginning at the lower third of the worksheet, draw a circle for the female and a square for the male, remembering not to make these symbols very large—a significant amount of information is yet to be compiled. Then connect them with a straight line across. Directly above each respective partner's symbol, repeat the previous pattern for each set of parents (remember: circles for females, squares for males) and connect each parent set with their child using a straight vertical line.

Next, insert symbols for all siblings (including step- and half-siblings) of the prospective spouses on the line that connects the parents, maintaining a left-to-right progression of oldest to youngest, repeating the process for their parent's siblings. At this point, it is advisable to inquire about their parents' parents and include any member thought to be influential. Lest we forget, the structure of the genogram's constituency is a product of what each partner views as useful or memorable. We have co-constructed genograms extending to three or four generations of exceptional individuals many, many times!

Once the basic outline has been completed, you can begin to gather information about the couple's family. We have found it easiest to begin with what may be thought of as the factual aspects of their families. Facts are those events of family life that are verifiable and consensual such as ages, birth dates, occupations, levels of education, marriages and remarriages, divorces, and deaths. While there is an endless amount of facts available to couples, this information is not always immediately accessible. The fact-gathering aspect of the premarital interview sometimes requires each partner talking to and about members of their family from whom they have not heard for some time. We always allow the couple the opportunity to "fill in the blanks" as the availability of information evolves.

Next, begin to identify those individual family members who have been or are successfully functioning with respect to occupation, marriage, health, and relationships. This information can be recorded on the genogram worksheet and may also include any brief emotional, behavioral, or medical descriptions of individuals. The value of this exercise will emerge during subsequent sessions when premarital participants begin to identify and relate to those family members' stories and experiences.

Last, a graphic representation of family relationships as interpreted by the couple should be noted on the worksheet. The symbols used here are understandably arbitrary and represent a shorthand method for identifying interpersonal relationships by visually connecting family members; if these don't work for you, make up your own. What we are primarily concerned with is not the symbols themselves but how potential questions are framed and offered to the couple. The following represents how we form our questions and the symbols or lines we use:

Question	Symbol
"Is there anyone in your families who…	
gets along well with (one or both of) you?"	+ + +
gets in trouble or likes to argue with you?"	_ _ _
is your favorite, or someone you admire a lot?"	! ! !
you do not wish to see very much at all?"	x x x
you wish you could get to know better?"	)))

Constructing genograms can become somewhat complex and confusing, especially if there are such things as multiple marriages, major events, or differing perspectives. If it becomes apparent that more than one worksheet is needed for each segment of genogram construction, feel free to improvise and implement them. While we cannot anticipate all the contingencies, we suggest that during the "getting to know you" phase, some general questions regarding each partner's family will give a helper a preview for the nature and scope of their genogram's assembly.

It is important to note that the "map is not the territory" (Korzybski 1973) when utilizing genograms in the context of a competency approach to premarital work. These descriptive tools potentially serve many functions, not the least of which entail the interpersonal empowering of people's sense of history and future. We unabashedly avoid utilizing genograms to "problem-make" historical influences. Above all else, our approach remains the same with any assessment process: maintain curiosity, listen actively, and never rest in your quest to heighten your awareness of a couple's relationship strengths and resources.

As we stated above, we consistently strive to implement competency-based conversations during the premarital interview. In addition to intergenerational topics, couples usually raise subjects that appear, at first hearing, substantial but somewhat vague. These topics, for example, could be as varied as leisure time, communication, finances, or feeling states. Our experience with these types of observations has lead us to use what are generally termed "scaling" questions (de Shazer 1994). The net effect of such questions is to make more tangible that which is sometimes hard to describe so that goals may be established. In addition, these questions open the conversation up for further inquiry about said observations. Typically, the 0-to-10 scale is used and resembles the following: *Let's say that 0 stands for when you guys first met and 10 stands for what each of you hope (the relationship, communication, etc.) will be at its very best. Where would you say you are between 0 and 10 today?* Upon receiving their numerical response a follow up question might be: *How much work was it to arrive at (this number)? Given this amount of satisfaction what will it take to continue on to (the next higher number)? How will you know when you arrive at (this number)? What will you be doing differently then? How will your partner know?* Lest it go unsaid, we do not take a Pollyanna stance with regards to relationship quality—not every relationship will reach or stay at a 10. To encourage honesty and thoughtful consideration, we will at some point offer the following: *It's highly likely that with any relationship there will be some normal fluctuation and so I was wondering: If the [relationship, etc.] stayed around a __, would that be satisfactory for the both of you?* .

In closing, we do not want you, the helper, to think that scaling numbers are anything more than a simple way to dialogue about the concerns expressed by the people with whom you are working. If our approach to premarital work has raised your interest in how to illuminate resources, then we have been successful.

MAKING GOOD GROWTH SENSE: CELL MINISTRY IN THE CHURCH

Nothing is more important for teaching us to understand the concepts we have acquired than constructing some fictitious ones.

—Wittgenstein

A Story

A long time ago there was a boy who sat on a riverbank in the company of an older and, from the boy's perspective, much wiser man than most he had ever met. After a short while, a series of faint honking noises from up the river began to grow louder and louder with more accompanying honks as a big white moving "V" approached. The boy asked the older man what it was about that peculiar "V" formation that geese apparently appreciated so much.

The older man looked at the boy and said, "Well, I can't speak for the geese, but this is what makes sense to me. As near as I can figure, each time the bird flaps its wings, it creates a lifting effect for the bird immediately following. By flying in a V shape they get a greater flying range than if they were to fly on their own."

"Oh, I see, " said the boy, and as boys are apt to do, he asked another question of the older man. "What happens when they get tired?" he asked.

"Well, whenever a goose falls out of formation, it feels the weight of trying to do it alone, and quickly gets back into the V to take advantage of the lifting power of the bird immediately in front. When the lead goose gets tired, he moves back into the V, and another goose flies point."

"Gee whiz," said the boy, "it makes you think about what hard work it must be to get to where they want to go."

"Yes, it surely does," said the older man, "but let me tell you something else I have noticed over the years. When a goose gets sick or is wounded by a hunter and falls out, two geese fall out of formation and follow him down to help and protect him. They stay with him until he is able to fly, or until he is dead. Then they launch out with another formation so they can catch up with their group."

"Oh," said the boy now noticeably less excited.

"Is there anything else you would like to talk about?" asked the older man now a little concerned over his little friend's subdued demeanor.

"Yes, I was wondering about something. Do you think that when geese do all that honking they are really encouraging the other geese in the group?"

"Well, frankly, son, I don't speak goose," the old man said, "but it seems a little goose reassurance goes a long way."

We employ this illustration after having read several dozen books on church growth, leadership, mentoring, and other related topics. We were struck by the unique approaches taken in each book, their varying degrees of complexity, and the exceptional attention to detail, especially when documenting what apparently happens as a result of following their lead. As meaningful as these ideas were, however, we were left with a nagging sense of fatigue after making sense of all the complexities involved in growing people. As a result, a different description of how people develop growth relationships in a group context was needed. And just as the above story indicated, the geese flying in the "V" relationship possessed more than just a potent flying formation or an acute affiliation based on travel needs. The geese in question, by their very natures, were authentically interested in seeing that every member of the group contributed to and completed the journey set before them. Using aspects of the above illustration, we will touch on some useful orientations concerning small-group or cell growth.

Cells in the Church

A significant change has taken place in church ministry across the world as congregations have moved away from being program-driven to what George (1994, 63) calls "relationship-driven" bodies, empowering people to use their gifts in community (cf. Wilson et al. 1993). George's excellent book on church growth places emphasis on cells or small ministry groups within the larger congregation. "A cell is a place where people have enough social reference points to find themselves sustained emotionally and spiritually" (p. 69), and the primary focus in this type of congregational organization is effective functioning of individuals in close community. The cell philosophy revolves around the managed leader, a person who functions as the group's guide and facilitator under the supervision of another. Central to George's cell philosophy is docent organization; that is, a person becomes a disciple with the understanding that he or she will also take up a leadership responsibility as soon as possible. Supervision of each cell leader from the paid staff outward is an ongoing part of the church growth process.

Competency-mindedness is a great fit with cell philosophy in the church. For the church leader seeking more effective ministry as well as higher minister-to-member ratios, combining the competency view with cell organization is a natural because they can share many of the same assumptions about change, growth, and giftedness. For example, George (1994) states that the best way for leadership to develop is to move away from the teach-assign-do progression to one that emphasizes assign-do-teach. Within this approach, members identify their personal strengths and gifts and are asked to take on tasks that fit naturally (as opposed to seeking out members when a position needs to be filled with a warm body). When a member begins a task or ministry, she or he moves into performing the tasks of the position with as little training and education as possible, as it is assumed that each person will seek counsel and request instruction when needed. So, rather than assuming that members are deficient and in need of education before beginning ministry, they are seen as having "different gifts, according to the grace given us" (Romans 12:6), competent and coached in the process of ministering. Congruent with the tenets of competency-based therapy, George suggests that the in-motion member be approached by the supervisor with the following question: "What would you like to learn about how to do your responsibility better?" (p.78).

Not every church has implemented (or should implement) a cell philosophy. It seems, however, that ideas from this approach to church growth can be adapted to meet the needs, goals, and calling of any congregation. We would suggest several competency-based supervision ideas for your consideration as you develop new, more effective leaders in your setting.

We believe that curiosity and respect should be at the forefront of any relationship-based approach to leadership development. The old "top-down" philosophy of leadership might work well in the military, but most who write and speak in organizational philosophy today favor a center-out or collaborative approach to building cooperation in voluntary and business groups. From the supervision experiences of young therapists (Heath and Tharp 1991) come the following ideas, which we have found to be invaluable in creating a cooperative context. First, persons in supervision request relationships based on *mutual* honor, to hold and to be held in high regard. Also, people do not expect their supervisors to be "gurus." This implies that supervisors do not have to know everything and that collegiality is valued more than hierarchy. Next, persons in supervision ask that supervisors assume that they are competent, as they are usually harsh critics of their own performance already. It is common knowledge that people thrive on affirmation and feel empowered when supervisors tell them what they are doing *right*; what is unfortunate is that we use this philosophy successfully with young children but fail to apply it through the lifespan. Finally, persons in supervision want supervisors to listen. Just as clients are the experts on their own experience, we believe that persons-in-ministry have a valid viewpoint of their performance and the supervisor's view is not superior. For supervisors to listen to those entrusted to their care is not a tremendous complement; it is also necessary in order to be of service and build relationship trust.

Several other ideas may be helpful in guiding one to more effective supervisory relationships. In keeping with George's (1994) assumption that effective functioning should be a primary focus, one should attend to changing approaches to problems rather than highlighting personal attributes that seem problematic. Michael White and David Epston (1990) direct us to see that the person is not the problem in this approach—the *problem*, as it is storied and lived, is the problem. Most difficulties are best approached with a change in strategy; personality or philosophical changes to resolve a problem are not usually necessary (or achievable). Therefore, attention should be given to that which is changeable and possible rather than the intractable and hopeless. The supervisor's main task is to identify and amplify positive change and success (see Thomas 1996). Supervisors continually make choices based on what they believe is most important to attend to. Being continuously aware of the fact that there are many "right" ways of ministering to the needs of others, effective leaders focus on what is going well rather than on correcting and attempting to force compliance. The competency-based supervisor encourages continued success, uncovering small accomplishments and highlighting capabilities as a major part of the training process.

With these guiding ideas in mind, we believe the approaches outlined in chapter 3 are very helpful in developing competent leadership. Setting achievable goals, identifying exceptions to problems, accessing personal resources, using presuppositional language, and using future-oriented questions are all adaptable for use outside the counseling context. For example, let's consider a new supervisory relationship. After identifying her spiritual and developed gifts through your new member class, Dale has agreed to apply herself to the task of church visitor follow-up. Dale throws herself into her duties and, according to her fellow committee members and returning visitors, she has been very effective in engaging people and creating a spirit of welcome. You want your first monthly supervisory meeting to go well, but you are concerned about the amount of time she is spending away from her family as she accomplishes her tasks. The following dialogue exemplifies a competency approach:

Pastor: I have heard wonderful things about your work! How have you managed to do so much in such a short period of time? (*Complimenting achievements, seeking Dale's understanding of her performance*)

Dale: Well, I work hard, and I have a knack for getting people to feel "at home."

Pastor: How do you do that? I'm curious. (*Seeking to be informed as a fellow learner*)

Dale: (*Responds with specifics*)

Pastor: When looking at our church and committee goals for visitation, how well do you think you're doing? Maybe using a "0 to 10" scale would help—let's say "0" is "I'm a miserable failure" (which we both know isn't true!) and "10" is "There is no way I could improve"—where would you put your accomplishments? (*Use of scaling technique, emphasis on the positive achievements*)

Dale: I'd say I'm about at a "7" right now.

Pastor: Wow! You know, I'd have to rank you at a "7" or higher, from what I've seen and heard. This is a great start! Now, is there anything I can do to help you improve from that "7" to, say, an "8"?

Dale: Well, I wish I could see more people. It seems that when I spend more time with a person or family, they are more likely to return. But I'm just out of time!

Pastor: I'd like to help with that. Let's explore it a little. How much time do you normally spend with a visitor when you go to the home? What do you talk about? How did you decide to talk about that? (*Highlights Dale's expertise, explores her experience respectfully, allows the pastor to be a learner*)

Dale: (*Gives detailed response*)

Pastor: Can you recall a time recently when you spent less time with a visitor, and he or she came back to worship? (*Explores exceptions*)

Dale: Well, yes—Mr. and Mrs. Rodriguez came back the last three weeks, and my first visit with them was only ten minutes! I just didn't have the time to spend that day because I had to get my dog to the vet for surgery. They did stop after the service this week and tell me how much my visit encouraged them to return.

Pastor: What did you do during that ten minutes that made such a difference? (*Explores the exception, enhancing existing success*)

Dale: (*Responds with a description of how she "compacted" her usual questions, information, and greetings*)

Pastor: Listen—I'm interested in accomplishing the goals of the church; at the same time, I want to support you so you can labor effectively for as long as you want without burning out! Now, are there ways we can think of together that might allow you to take that "compacted" approach and be just as effective so you spend a little less time at this?

Another example to emphasize personal resources and realistic goal setting may be helpful. Dante, a young college student who has grown up in the congregation, has volunteered to be one of the worship leaders for the weekly children's church service. He is one of six children's church leaders who meet regularly together and rotate Sundays, allowing for creativity to evolve. You are the supervisor, a Christian Education minister who meets monthly with each leader. The agreed-upon goal is to move toward a docent relationship with Dante, who will then supervise these worship leaders on an ongoing basis. After beginning with questions highlighting successes and positive change, the dialogue might continue in this vein:

Pastor: So, what is it about you that has allowed these successes to happen? (*Highlighting personal resources*)

Dante: I just give all the credit to God. God is my inspiration. God told me I could best serve with the children, so, here I am!

Pastor: I couldn't agree more. God certainly has used you as a vessel in wonderful ways. So, why did God choose you? What gifts has God given you that allow for the best ministry for these kids?

Dante: I have a special love for children, I know that. I also love to sing, and I guess I'm a natural storyteller!

Pastor: I wish I could be there to hear them! How do you express this special love for children during the service? I mean, if I was sitting with the children, what would I see and hear?

Dante: (*Gives detailed description of his actions, with prompting*)

Pastor: Did you know that you could do all of these things before you started leading worship for the children? . . . How did you know that? . . . What other ways have you found to use these resources? (*Seeking historical information on his personal resources, pointing out his giftedness and personal knowledge about these talents*)

Dante: (*Responds, a bit embarrassed at taking credit for his strengths*)

Pastor: Now, I don't know if I can be of help, but most of the time, people find that a good way to improve is to set goals. What would you think of looking toward the future for a moment?

Dante: OK.

Pastor: Imagine a future in which you are leading the worship services, and they are now the best they could ever be. This means they fit with the children's needs, God's desires, and the goals our congregation has prayerfully set. What is happening? What are you continuing to do that you are already doing? (*Defines success as collaborative change, concentrates on what Dante is already contributing rather than what he is not doing*)

Dante: (*Describes his vision*)

Pastor: That's great. I like the sound of that, and I'm sure God would be pleased. Now, what would be a small step in that direction, to make that happen? How could I help you make that first step?

In this example, the pastor fits with Dante's language, accesses personal resources, and makes a step toward setting achievable goals. It is respectful of Dante's worldview and focuses on learning more than teaching. Most of all, this example brings out the necessity for collaboration when working in a supervisory relationship. Dante brought his own style, view, and gifts to the position, which means he does it as no other can. Because it is easier to steer a moving vehicle than stop it, supervision revolves around small course changes to empower Dante's own change process. In addition, the pastor is modeling a style that Dante might adopt for his future supervisory relationships, as it is both adaptable and personal.

In the broadest sense, our competency-based approach to working with people has to do with flying. We are not suggesting that church staff or members try to leave the ground; rather, we are addressing the role and interaction of church staff and their relationships with congregational participants. Perhaps an example will assist in highlighting what we mean.

It was to be an exciting Sunday. All the numbers were in and everyone eagerly awaited the results. The success of the food drive was a vital part of the youth and mission committee's goals to reach a designated group of people who were themselves attempting to start a small mission effort. As the Sunday school hour began, staff members would drop by and speak to everyone about the hard work and the abundant outcome. Unfortunately, in the midst of the appropriate accolades being paid to the volunteer participants, the primary emphasis appeared to underscore the apparent effectiveness of the staff's perseverance and performance. The sermon that Sunday focused on the necessity of church ministry to guide the congregation into more such successful endeavors, the result of which would be reflected in the increased number of outreach groups and missionary churches in the area. Upon leaving the service people could be overheard saying something to the effect that "it is good to know that we can rely upon our ministers and staff to pull through when we need them."

It is fortunate that most churches have trained and capable staff. But before reading the preceding chapters, how many might be persuaded that the norm for many staff and member interactions revolves around what we have discussed as an "expert" position? That is to say, there exists an individual expert somewhere in the church structure who proposes actions to be taken in a particular area of concern by grouping individuals together, formulating a goal, deciding on a plan of action, then moving toward that goal. While a competency-based approach to ministry recognizes this function of staff ministry in the offering of direction and support as viable, it generally fails to be a developer of people. It is our bias that those groups which applaud the minister's performance while not empowering the members will not get small-group activity to take off and fly effectively. From our experience as staff members, maintaining the "expert" frame of reference as a minister is a substantial factor in perpetuating the proverbial "spectator" position so common with church participation. One of the reasons we think that the latter condition is the norm and not the exception is that it is easier to become entranced with matters related to organization and polity than training, equipping, and empowering people to be inventive.

Within our approach, church staff can begin eliciting a new frame of consultation or, as is common with counseling help staff, one of supervision. As stated by George (1994), "Most churches would be more effective if they shifted from being orientation heavy to being supervision heavy" (p. 83). Supervision develops more accountability inside and outside a group's framework and the related formulation of goals associated with that particular group. Our approach to supervising closely adheres to the assumptions about clients we have outlined previously. In other words, the emphasis is invited to shift from "There is only one way (the right way) to do this" to "Which way would work for you in light of your interests, calling, or leading?" and "What are you already doing well that might assist others with this————?" Again, as a reminder, these are general observations that may be utilized in many contexts but serve to underscore our firm belief that churches that favor supervision of participants instead of a ponderous "platform" will find themselves to be far more effective. The results of implementing a competency stance have been as varied as these:

- Participants became more enchanted with developing their resources and abilities rather than merely promoting a Sunday school curriculum or program.
- Participants helped others develop their gifts instead of increasing their dependency on a staff expert to lead the way.
- Paid staff consistently found novel methods of encouraging and developing volunteer leaders.

A lesson from our goose story involves the moving body of geese and the difficulty, if not the undesirability, of going it alone. As mentioned earlier, when one flyer begins to bear the weight of solo flight, he or she quickly moves back into the path of maximum cooperation. Applying this idea to competency-based interaction suggests that any effective group activity will be reflected when individual members move in concert with others in the group. This requires, however, a spoken and realistic consensus of activities and goals for the group. A competency-based approach might evaluate individual goal formulation and ask, "It sounds as if your goal of ———— is clear. If you were successful in getting this idea across to others, what would that look like? If not, what might you consider changing about your personal goal with respect to the group's goals? What would be the first indication that the group is beginning to getting on track with these ideas?" As stated earlier, goals are more readily transacted if they can be corroborated by other members. As in all group applications, goal negotiation is likely to succeed when vague feelings, thoughts, or behaviors are replaced with clearly articulated goals that are more pragmatic and (it is hoped) more useful. That way the participants, like the geese in our example, can operate in the group and stay abreast of those who are steering their course in a unified effort.

Our story also involves the head goose tiring and dropping back into the formation so as to allow another to take the lead. For those experimenting with competency ideas this might be best translated as letting others take turns with the more demanding interactions of a particular group. This will be difficult for those to whom the expert role has been benevolently assigned or for those inclined to adopt the lead goose position as the only desirable or viable posture to assume in a group effort. When lay groups have a perpetual head, there is often an underlying idea that to relinquish the leader role would be to admit failure, and avoiding embarrassment becomes a defining concern of the group and the leader. This is especially problematic if this idea is tied up with performance-based interactions with people in relationship. A competency-based approach would acknowledge that participants may not intentionally put pressure on a leader to perform but might express implicitly the demand, "Do something leader!" Thus, an artificial barrier is created to viewing relationships any other way because one is in possession of the "right" way. Thinking back to our earlier discussion of frames and their usefulness, one might be reminded of the notion that frames serve functions, not all of which are expedient in resolving dilemmas in human interaction. Regarding the leader frame of reference in terms of group function, we have observed that people left to their own devices will define themselves as leaders or followers. This appears to be a natural by-product of our propensity for creating a system of hierarchy. The mistake made here, as elsewhere, is that the ease of instituting hierarchical metaphors does not always justify their implementation. Within a competency frame, we would remind members that it is never "either/or," but "both/and." This is exemplified by our leader-and-follower notion, for if one is pressed it becomes difficult, if not impossible, to discern which comes first or where one would be without the other. It appears salient to establish a plan of rotation within each particular group that revolves memberships in and out of leadership positions so that the acting leader does not get his goose cooked!

Now, what to do about all that honking? It should be clear that one will probably never know the "why" of the honking. The meaning of the message is the response you get. Focusing on cooperative models and encouraging collaboration among competent members will result in the removal of restraints and empowered membership . . . and aren't results more important than knowing "why"?

"WELL, WELL, WELL"[2]:
DISCOVERING HOW HEALTH CREATES MORE HEALTH
IN THE DEVELOPMENT OF FAMILY WELLNESS

Each of us has had opportunities to speak to lay audiences on the topic of "family values." Knowing that this important issue has been usurped by American political figures does not diminish its importance in the life of the church, where families have always been valued. The problem is always the same: How do we speak about "health" or "wellness" when we have no touchstone or set of guiding ideas about it? Psychiatry, pastoral counseling, and family therapy all claim to address various pathologies in family life, but who speaks for health?

Here is an example of how a focus on family wellness in a parish setting can be valuable in both the vibrance of the church and the expectations parishioners bring to counseling. I (FNT) was hired by a ministerial alliance to speak to a citywide audience. I chose the topic "Finding the Positives in Your Family." It was a congenial crowd, and as the time flew by, the smiles and conversations became brighter and brighter. I simply outlined several concepts—including the categories called "communication" and "connectedness/spirituality" in this chapter—and then divided the audience into groups of six to eight members each (keeping families together whenever possible). I guided the audience members into vocalizing positive stories that illustrated their family health in spite of the pressure we all feel to focus on what is wrong with our relationships. It was a smashing success! In fact, when the time was up, many people stayed in their newly-formed groups with folks they had never met before and continued the sharing process with substantial laughter! It was a speaker's dream—I got the ball rolling, and the crowd found great value in the "message" they—not I—had supplied. When given the chance to focus on what is right in their lives, people can develop meaningful experiences that can be tapped in Sunday school, family life education, and youth work.

We believe that families should define their own dreams and goals around the issue of health. When others define how a family "should" be, they inevitably limit rather than expand the family's choices. Even though people in the U.S. continue to call for a "return to family values," there never seems to be an unchanging, clearly defined "place" to return to. Stephanie Coontz has written a scholarly yet readable book titled *The Way We Never Were: American Families and the Nostalgia*

Trap (1992). Coontz carefully documents family trends around working women, divorce, sex, class problems, and family self-reliance, and reveals a very different 1950s and 1960s American culture and family life from that portrayed by politicians, media, and even church leaders. The difference revolves around myth and memory—since we cannot return to the past, it is open to reconfiguration and quickly moves from recollection to a real, concrete "what was." Coontz writes, "Not all myths are bad, of course. People need shared stories and rituals to bring them together and reinforce social solidarity. But myths that create unrealistic expectations about what families can or should do tend to erode solidarities and diminish confidence in the problem-solving abilities of those whose families 'fall short'" (p. 6).

In keeping with our themes and assumptions, we firmly believe that each family is unique and therefore requires vision, form, values, and habits that are uniquely its own. Of course, there will be overlap with other families because of shared socioeconomic status, culture, history, religion, and so on. But this cannot diminish the necessity of ownership and agency when people consider the question, "Are we a healthy family?" We outline a few ideas here in hopes of creating a parallel process between the counseling setting and the home. Following this, you will find several areas of family life that lend themselves to analysis. With these focal areas in mind, we believe readers will find multiple applications in preaching, teaching, and self-guided discussion with their own families.

First, families are the experts on their own "brand" of health. Because we do not believe that problems define families, we hold to the idea that most families are capable of defining their own ways of being and are more likely to be motivated when intervention or new information heads them in directions they want to go. "One of the main effects of problems, and peoples' experience of them, is to blind people from noticing their strengths and capabilities" (Durrant 1995, 13). Families have within them a wealth of resources, both known and unknown to them, and the best way for a family to move forward into continued health is to utilize existing strengths, focus on successes in the past, and cooperate with their own competence. Therefore, our primary goal as educators, leaders, pastors, and counselors is to empower families to identify and access existing resources.

Some might say that this view is naive at best and possibly dangerous. One might remind us of domineering parents, abusive situations (sexual, physical, and emotional), oppressive relationships, and so on, and state that giving such families permission to remain isolated in their self-definition will be harmful. Although all of these thoughts warrant examination, we firmly believe that families will define themselves in ways congruent with their *past*, their *historical understanding of themselves*, and their *norms or values*, no matter how often "experts" attempt to "educate" them about "correct" ways of being a family. Because we do not believe that problems define families, we believe that the family is best approached with an assumption of self-rule, self-definition, and health because it gives them permission to focus on what is *right*, which is more likely to lead to changes in areas they find problematic than brow-beating and pathologizing. Problems do not indicate pathology—they are just one way of viewing things. When we view families as "problems" or as having "issues," we often respond as such and teach them to be incompetent in solving their own problems. A "deficiency" often says more about the observer making the statement than about the family. Remember the words of Ortega y Gassett: "Tell me to what you pay attention and I will tell you who you are." Therefore, instead of seeing a competency approach as endorsing abusive or extreme oppression, we believe that enhancing views of health are likely to promote discussions that lead to increased options in family life, including options that allow for humane and nonviolent family relationships. "People are generally better persuaded by the reasons which they have themselves discovered than by those which have come into the minds of others" (Pascal).

Continua of Family Health

"Health" is often pinpointed by outside experts and families alike on a line of pathology. That is, if you were to visually portray health, it might look something like this:

<—PATHOLOGICAL——>healthy<——PATHOLOGICAL—>

Such a scale only leads to the promotion of pathology, since so very few families will fit onto that dot labeled "healthy." Instead, consider the possibility that health can be everything *between* two extreme points of pathology:

pathological<————————>HEALTHY<————————>pathological

Like blood pressure, group dynamics, church size, and conversational content, health can just as easily be understood as a broad range of ways of belonging and being with a few ways of relating on the extreme ends of the range that tend to be problematic. How we came to understand constructs such as "mental health" and "health" as being so narrow that few ever achieve it is best left up to those who prefer archives and autopsies; for the rest of us, focusing on possibilities of positive change are more useful areas of focus and emphasis. We present three specific areas of family life based on family health research to provide focal points of discussion with families. Ways of opening up family dialogue are as varied as the imagination.

Family Communication

Consider the following concepts in graphic form. Ways of conceptualizing extremes that might not work well for families are on the ends; how families work out their own healthfulness can fall anywhere between the extremes.

Totally Covert ———————————————————— **Totally Overt**

For some families, teasing, playfulness, and other covert ways of communicating are vital to health. In others, such activity can be experienced as confusing or demeaning. Of course, if certain styles or methods of communicating harm a family member, they should be discussed and a preferred method created that is better for all parties involved. Every family can adjust to a more comfortable place on the continuum if solution-oriented family conversations align members to what feels *best* for each relationship.

Questions to facilitate conversation: *When am I communicating well with you? What do I do that helps us keep in close touch? What do you like about the way we talk with one another? When things are great regarding how we all communicate, what's happening? What are the special things you never want to lose regarding how you and _____ (Mom, Dad, Grandma, Susan, etc.) communicate? When is your communication clearest to you? What do you want to see continue in the way you and _____ communicate without words?*

Selfish Talker ———————————————————————— Selfish Listener

Somewhere along the way, these roles got polarized. In this concep-
tualization, both extremes can become problematic. It is necessary to
discover ways to talk and listen that are experienced as positive, since
every family is comfortable with different patterns.

Questions to facilitate conversation: *How am I listening to you
when you feel special? When you know I'm listening to you, what am I
doing so you know that? Do I talk too much most of the time I'm with
you, or not enough? When do you feel I'm doing a good job of balancing
talking and listening? How comfortable is our family with silences in
our conversations?*

Total Disclosure ———————————————————————— Total Secrecy

Most family experts would agree that secrecy in families should be
kept to a minimum. Disclosure can be used, however, as a means of
insuring conformity, gathering "ammunition" for future arguments, or
creating an imbalance of power. In our approach, family members
would discuss what parts of their lives are public (that is, open to discussion) and which parts are private. We prefer the words "private" and
"public" because they remove the negative meaning most people have
placed on the word "secrecy" when it is used in reference to family
communication. It is obvious to us that parents need to be age-appro-
priate, as certain areas of a child's life must be known to parents regardless of the child's desires. (For example, if a child is being harmed by
another adult, that is an area the child should always relate to the
parent[s].)

When it comes to communication, Americans seem to hold the
same attitude that they have regarding the acquisition and consump-
tion of goods: *more is better.* Anthropologist Ray Birdwhistell (1974)
conducted research on communication in stable marriages. The relationships he studied were identified as "stable" both by the couples and
by those who knew the couples well. A voice-sensitive audio tape
recorder was attached to each person, and they wore these devices for a
month prior the start of the study in order to become desensitized to
the intrusion. Then, Birdwhistell began recording and analyzing each
couple's communication patterns. He found that each couple in these
"good" relationships averaged only twenty-seven minutes of dyadic

conversation *per week!* His conclusion (and ours) is that satisfying, healthy communication is not a matter of "how much" but "how," "what," and "who." Part of what needs to be considered is when to make one's private thoughts available to one's family.

We routinely keep things to ourselves that should not become public. According to a "marriage breakers" list we found on the Internet, one question that spouses are told never to answer is, "If I died, would you remarry?" If one responds affirmatively, the spouse who raised the question might ask, "Am I that easy to replace?" If one answered "No," the questioner might respond, "Don't you like being married?" Another question to avoid is, "Am I too fat to wear this _____?" A "no" response might lead to this question: "You mean you'd let me out in public wearing something this tight?" If one were to reply with "Yes," then there is little doubt that the spouse could take offense at one's lack of tact! Even if one has an opinion, perhaps the best choice in these situations would be to reply, "There is no way I can respond to that question in that form without risking hurt feelings. Is there another way to ask it, or can I just not respond?"

We all have attitudes and opinions—about a son's weight, a daughter's choice of music, how old the in-laws look, and so on. Learning when to withhold information is just as vital to good relationships as deciding when to reveal your opinion.

Questions to facilitate conversation: *What area of your life would you prefer not to discuss? What areas of my life would you like to know more about? When I keep something private, how do I let you know that it is important for this area to be unquestioned? How will you let me know that you want to know my opinion on something, even when it might not agree with your own? How much thought privacy is too much, to you? What kinds of things do adults keep private from kids, and kids from adults?*

Always Expressing Feelings ——————— Never Expressing Feelings

Somewhere on this continuum is a range of health, and it varies with every family experience. This distinction, along with the one that follows, seems to find its way into nearly every marital counseling case we have ever experienced, because people have strong opinions on "right" ways of communicating. We will avoid gender stereotyping here, as it tends to disrupt the pastor's listening process, but many "pop psychology" books create gender differences between genders along these lines. Rarely, for instance, do we find people complaining about the wife's inability to be different from the husband. Most complaints could be paraphrased as, "If (s)he were more like me in expression of feelings, we'd have no problems!" Difficulties can be created because people are pushed to be more like the other, and they can be developed when one forbids the other to express emotion in certain ways. For example, many people bring their spouses to counseling, complaining of the other's inability to express emotions and accusing the other of being "closed." Others present for counseling with the complaint that their partners never control their feelings, causing problems in the marriage because the others "wear their hearts on their sleeves."

Rational ———————————————————— **Intuitive, Affective**

The twin of the above continuum involves the most common distinction we encounter regarding problem-solving in marriage: placing value on rational responses that are (seemingly) rational and logical versus responses based on feelings and intuition. Again, many in our field have been persuaded that differences on this continuum are somehow genetic or primary gender characteristics, but we have found that rigid entrenchment on either end is just as easily tied to social expectations, marital differences, family of origin explanations, or personal values. Arguments continue for years because one spouse does not value the other's way of knowing, making sense, and creating meaning in a context of difference.

We would suggest that the healthiest family communication takes place when a balance is struck between extremes and each person's way of expressing and knowing is valued. When family members know that their personal approach to both perceiving and communicating will be honored, a richer style of communicating can be developed.

Consider the following questions and comments to spark conversation:

If I were to express a little more (less) emotion when we talk, would it be better? How do I let you know that I value your opinion? When do you notice that I'm being more intuitive (if the person is more analytic)? When do you notice that I'm being more logical (if the person is more affective)? Give me an example of a recent time when you have felt comfortable with the way I expressed my feelings.

We're sure you get the picture from the examples above. If one is consistent in applying this schema with families, then the following distinctions may also be useful for assessment, playful discussion, and intervention:

COMMUNICATION

Always Available	Never Available
Agree	Disagree
Chaotic	Rigid
(No Predictive Rules)	(Overly Predictive Rules)
Verbal	Nonverbal
All Negative Labels	All Positive Labels
Always Unique	Always the Same
Always Same Location	Always Different Locations
Always Must Talk at the Table	No Talking at the Table
(or some other specific place)	
Always Conform	Always Disqualify

Family Connectedness and Spirituality

Of the ten areas we have distinguished when considering family health, two other areas seem vital when considering family health from a competency perspective: connectedness and spirituality. How healthy families connect is as varied as world cultures; this requires the pastoral counselor to approach each with reverence and respect. We believe one of the greatest mistakes a counselor can make is to "play God" with a family, attempting to form them in his or her image rather than encouraging them to find their own balance and style.

Consider the following table, to be used in viewing families as resourceful and inventive rather than deficient and inadequate. Create your own questions, games, metaphors, and stories to approach family health, using the following areas as a starting point:

CONNECTEDNESS:

Total Individuation	Total Enmeshment
Alone	Everyone
Adults	Children

Emotions ————————————————————— Intellect

Female ——————————————————————— Male

Dependent ——————————————————— Independent

Enmeshed——————————————————— Disengaged

Smothered ——————————————————— Abandoned

Verbal ——————————————————————— Nonverbal

Overly Flexible ——————————————— Inflexible

Must be Negative ————————————— Must be Positive

Moral Rules Unquestioned ——————— No Family Code of Ethics

Excessive Physical Contact ——————— No Physical Contact

SPIRITUALITY

Fellowship ——————————————————— Alone with God

Community——————————————————— Personal Spiritual Life

Evangelist ———————————————————— Communicant

Self—————————————————————————— Others

Disbelief ——————————————————— Unwavering Belief

Atheistic ——————————————————— Religiously Fanatical

Totally Against ————————————————— Totally For

Undisciplined —————————————————— Disciplined

Boundless Spirituality ——————— Narrow Range of Spirituality
("All is Spiritual")

As you can see, we create a lot of space within which individual families can breathe, move, and have their being. When what is "healthy"
becomes a local phenomenon for each family in its living context, guidance often takes the form of illuminating strengths, pointing out ranges
of health that can be negotiated, and encouraging exploration for the
competent. If this proposal is too grand, just remember the famous
words of the mythical Freud in the hit series "Northern Exposure":
"It's just a *theory!*"

To close this very diverse chapter, please consider these thoughts on
the apparent fellowship experienced by our geese as one falls from the
formation. Reuben Welch, an experienced campus pastor, wrote an
excellent little book years ago entitled *We Really Do Need Each Other*
(1973). The closing story in this book is about a "Group and Inter-

personal Relations" class that decides to go for a hike together to close the class on a high note. The first hike was a disaster—the strong led and the weak failed to keep up, and the entire experience was painful and frustrating. Fortunately, this was not the way it ended; they decided to do it again, with new rules: "it was everybody go or nobody go and they were all going together." In his own poetic form, Dr. Welch writes:

> So they set the day
> and made the sandwiches
> and made the chocolate
> and brought the cold drinks
> and the back packs
> and they got all gathered up
> for the safari,
> and they started up the mountain.
> It took them four hours to make it to the top,
> and the water was all gone
> and the cold drinks were all gone
> and the sandwiches were all gone
> and the chocolate was all gone
> and the back packs were empty
> but they all made it,
> together.
> . . . Christian fellowship is no place
> for get in or get out—
> it's get in,
> get in . . .
> But no matter how long it takes us
> we've got to go together.
> Because that's how it is
> in the body of Christ.

7

A CAUTIONARY NOTE
TO "GO SLOWLY"

"I can't believe that!" said Alice.
"Can't you?" the Queen said in a pitying tone.
"Try again: Draw a long breath, and shut your eyes."
—Lewis Carroll, *Through the Looking Glass*

I certainly can't say that change is always for the better;
but what I can say is that improvement necessitates change.
—G.C. Lichtenberg, *The Little Book of Consolation*

I (FNT) was meeting recently with a minister I have had the privilege of training, and our conversation turned to the application of competency-based ideas in pastoral counseling. She is quite proficient in the competency-based models and has excelled in adding to her repertoire of skills over the past year; however, she expressed a concern that really caught my attention. She said, "You know, at times, I feel like I'm just a cheerleader." Although her counselees were very satisfied with their time with her, she was feeling as though the competency-based models were "shallow" and insubstantial. An individually trained counseling pastor for ten years, Shelley sheepishly admitted that she sometimes missed the "good old days" of meat-and-potatoes, issues- and pathology-driven pastoral counseling that was loaded with tears, painful insights, and painful self-discovery. She confided,

> Now, don't get me wrong. I love this way of working with people, as it's probably added a decade to my career (by avoiding burnout), but sometimes I feel like I'm just superficial when all I look at are strengths and resources with clients. I don't get to use all of my knowledge, such as personality theory, diagnosis and assessment, and intervention techniques. Sometimes, I feel as if I'm not a pastor to these people—I mean, I'm supposed to see spiritual issues in everyone, right?

125

Many practicing the ideas from this book may have similar feelings. Taking on the assumptions of our model of counseling—that counselees are the experts on their lives, that people have the resources necessary to resolve their problems, that people have moments of stuckness, and so on—may lead us to personally review past learning, practice, and assumptions. Your transition from intrapsychic conflicts to more solution-oriented, interactive views centered on problem resolution may result in conflictual thoughts. Am I doing enough? What if there really *is* something wrong with her thought processes? If he needs medication and I don't seek psychiatric consultation, could I harm him? Is this all there is to change? Could it be this simple?

GUARDING AGAINST POLLYANNA

As mentioned previously, Pollyanna's focus was blindly optimistic. A Pollyanna might continue resuscitation efforts on one who has been under water for hours, or fight to remove the "no code" notation from a terminally ill mother's chart. Such a person might tell everyone who wants to be president of the United States or play pro sports that they can do it, regardless of talent, ethnic origin, gender, or age. Pollyanna doesn't believe in limitations and always looks for the next miracle to overturn reality.

In our work with people in pastoral counseling situations, we have to deal with more than "hope that springs eternal"—we must confront the particulars of the person-in-context, who both has limitations and must live with the certainty of them. We do not deny that each person living on this planet is a finite human being with limited time and talents. But no one can know what is true about another person, and it is doubtful that one can be objective enough to know exactly what is true within one's own life. We believe that it is this *certainty of uncertainty* that opens up possibilities for pastoral couselors, clients, and the counseling context. It seems to us that change is limited more by people than by circumstances, and the competency-based model of pastoral counseling creates optimal conditions under which not-yet-conceived alternatives can be safely examined and undertaken by both helpers and counselees.

There are two risks involved in the "Pollyanna" idea. One is quite evident: It would be unethical to reinforce beliefs that are *totally* unrealistic. Pushing for change that cannot happen is to be avoided when practicing this model. Examples of Pollyann-ish errors abound: trying to undo the past; attempting to reexperience one's life; focusing on changing unchangeable circumstances (one's race or age, for example); or trying to change other people's views or beliefs. These are folly. To reinforce a counselee's idea that "all things are possible" without examining one's context is at best cruel and at worst harmful. We have never intended to promote a foolishly optimistic position as we developed our approach within this book. We believe that the *limits usually imposed upon therapeutic change are often created by counselees and pastoral counselors who aim too low and dream too little.* Rather than focusing on the "truth," we propose that everyone involved in the pastoral counseling process examine the *other* actualities—exceptions to problems, personal strengths, and contextual resources—that lead to new possibilities for change.

In addition, do we not hold to the belief that God is free to change people and experiences? Is the God of Israel shackled by our interpretation of history and experience? Is it not true that the Lord of life is able to influence beyond our own limited abilities to perceive and acknowledge? Whatever one's formal theology, the omnipotence of God must be examined; once it is considered, fewer limits are placed on possibility.

Most pastoral counselors, because of their desire to "do no harm," will err on the conservative side of this issue; that is, most of us restrain change in our practice style and philosophy because we were trained that change is arduous, slow, and painful and can fail. We often hold hypotheses well beyond their proven usefulness in the counseling setting, usually to the point where maintaining our beliefs may be ridiculous. Evidence in the efficacy of brief counseling abounds (Fisher 1980; Fisher 1984; Garfield 1980; Koss and Butcher 1986; Koss and Shiang 1994; Lambert, Shapiro, and Bergin 1986; Nardone and Watzlawick 1993), yet we sometimes hold to the theory that long-term counseling is more effective. Sometimes our counselees improve quickly, but, in spite of the experiential evidence, we find it difficult to believe that real change can happen "that fast." And we maintain beliefs in ways of conducting ourselves in counseling—such as insisting on the expert position—years beyond their necessity.

Two things come to mind. First, if you are struggling with some of the assumptions of our model of counseling, then join the club—we do, too. Making transitions from belief systems may be simple, but they may not be easy. We, too, encounter internal conflicts concerning accuracy and truth, and we haven't resolved them for ourselves yet; so, always keep in mind that we are all dealing with new information and strange encounters with the familiar rather than with conversion to a new religion. Second, we hope you will believe that your experiences with our model of counseling have validity. It has been our experience that our theories often impede therapeutic change; our ideas about change get in the way of actual change. If we believe that change simply cannot be as rapid or pervasive as it is experienced by the counselee, then our theory may interfere with and negate the reality of a lived difference. Alfred North Whitehead (cited in Bateson 1972) has often called attention to what he termed "misplaced concreteness," the logical error of believing that the thing and the name of the thing are the same. It is not uncommon to reify concepts that cannot be proven true. In our culture, we have elevated concepts such as "ego," "personality," "self," and other constructs to the position of truth on par with "chair," "bird," and "cloud"; that is, we often fail to distinguish thoughts from things. Clergy sometimes hold firmly to the tenets of a theory desipte the client's experience of change and the pastoral counselor's experience of a changed counselee. We hope that you will not be blindly optimistic that your *theory* of change is true in spite of the reality of change that surrounds you.

USING COUNSELEE FEEDBACK TO GUIDE YOUR PASTORAL COUNSELING

Ministers and counselors have always sought to understand the process of therapeutic change—and so have counselees! Descriptions of change from the counselor's viewpoint abound; we would venture to say that the essence of the publishing industry's relationship with counselors is found in the writings of "master" clinicians who publish books outlining the process of change from one side of counseling's recursive experience. One of us (Thomas 1994) has written on alternative descriptions of change from counselees' viewpoints, and many mental health colleagues around the country are employing approaches such as this in counseling research (Barnard and Kuehl 1995, Kuehl 1987, Mabery 1993, Metcalf 1993, Newfield et al. 1990, Quinn 1998, Swint 1994). We believe it is necessary to discuss ways to access counselee viewpoints so you will be able assess your work and improve your skills. Since we believe the counselee is the expert on his or her experience, this includes the pastoral counseling experience. Remember: you know not because you ask not!

We frequently ask counselees to let us know their experiences of counseling, attempting to comprehend the experience of the counselee(s) and utilizing this to inform our follow-up contacts with the counselee and future work with other counselees. You may find some of the following questions helpful as you access this important source of information:

Global:

- *How did we do today?*
- *Overall, how are we doing together?*
- *How do you think counseling has been going, to this point?*
- *Is counseling with me what you expected it would be?*
- *What has been helpful to you so far?*

Specific:

- *Is there anything important that I missed today?*
- *What was helpful today? Could you be specific?*
- *Was I "on target" today? In what area?*
- *What is the most helpful thing we did today?*
- *If you were to describe what went well today in our time together, what would you say?*

Although it seems to be common sense, few pastoral counselors we talk to have a clear idea of what their counselees value in the counseling process. We have found that taking a few minutes each session to discuss this as well as spending a bit more time on it when counselees conclude their counseling can be very helpful in several ways. Such information cannot be obtained from workshops, books, classes, or other professionals—it is specific to *your* style and *your* counselees. What you receive is an alternative version of a piece of your own history, creating a "binocular view" (Bateson 1979, 33) through the contrast that is highly informative and beneficial for current counseling approaches.

We would suggest that you take notes as your clients relate their experience of pastoral counseling with you. Whether you write down important material before, during, or after a contact with a client is up to you. Make it a part of the specific file as well as your global assessment of your work, and allow it to become a routine way of informing your work. We often videotape termination interviews in which the counselee relates his or her experience in counseling. These extended descriptions often allow counselees to review the overall experience of change, and the focus is usually on how they have altered their present and created a hopeful future. After we finish, we give the videotape to the counselee(s) for their future reference, adding that they might want to review the tape "if they need reminding of their terrific progress." This often serves as a diary or journal for parishioners, allowing them to reexamine their experience with a focus on transformation.

However this is accomplished—through written feedback, oral interviews, or simple end-of-session questions—counselees' viewpoints should inform what we do if we take the foundational ideas of competency-based counseling seriously. Yes, this is research. Yes, this will take some of our valuable time. However, we have found the return to be enormously helpful in guiding our work with counselees as we move toward problem resolution and as we evaluate our personal skills and orientation in this counseling model.

HOW TO AVOID BECOMING A "SOLUTION-FORCED" PASTORAL COUNSELOR

Working within CBC models for years has certainly created a prejudice in us. We prefer pastoral counseling with an orientation toward positive change; however, there are times when such an approach can be misapplied. Several articles (Efron 1994, Efron and Veenendaal 1993, Friedman 1993, Nylund and Corsiglia 1994, Simon 1994) have been appropriately critical of this approach, and there will no undoubtedly be others. Bradford Keeney, one of the finest minds in psychotherapy today, reminds us that *all* counseling models and approaches were invented, not discovered (Keeney 1988). From Freud to Rogers, Minuchin to de Shazer, and Oates to Stone, every model began as a tentative map to guide the pastoral counselor through unique and challenging counseling situations. And rather than ask, "Does this model work with this presenting problem?" those inventors instead asked, "How do we make this model work in this situation?" For the eclectic as well as for the model purist, we constantly seek new ways to adapt our maps to real life. Remember, "the map is not the territory."

Nylund and Corsiglia (1994) remind us that competency-based counseling models are helpful guides, but we must honor the counselees' experiences and tailor our approaches if we are to be successful. They point out three specific misapplications that should (and can) be avoided. First, our model of pastoral counseling does not insist that only "solution talk" is permitted. Some pastoral counselors force solution talk on clients who, for a variety of reasons, are not responsive to such an approach. If counselees are constrained from meaningful expression or compelled to talk in a particular fashion, they will oppose our attempts with equal efforts, resulting in what Keeney (1983) has called symmetrical escalation. First and foremost, pastoral counselors must attend to the immediate contextual clues of success or obstruction. As the old saying goes, God gave us two ears and one mouth for a reason!

Second, some pastoral counselors have the mistaken idea that every "exception" is of equal importance. Durrant and Kowalski (1990) have warned us that:

> It is important not to convince clients that exceptions are significant. Attempting to convince often amounts to an irresistible invitation to argue even more strongly for the abuse [problem]-dominated view. Rather, we find it helpful to adopt a stance of curiosity and ask questions that invite clients to entertain ideas of personal agency. (p. 93).

Michael White (1991) reminds us that "for an event to comprise a unique outcome (or exception), it must be qualified as such by the persons to whose life the event relates" (p. 30). Therefore, it is not so much what the pastor sees as significant but what the counselee views as critical in importance. We have both experienced and witnessed solution-forcing counseling in this form. What can be observed in such instances is a pastor who has forgotten his or her primary goal: to allow the counselees to be the experts on their lived experience. When this is set aside in favor of model specificity, counselees often become frustrated with both the person and the process of counseling and fail to engage or continue.

Many competency-based pastoral counselors view all exceptions as doorways to success instead of allowing the counselee/counselor interaction to elicit the optimal choice(s). For example, Joan (age thirty-five) was having nightmares, wetting the bed, and struggling with her relationship with her mother. Given this wide range of problems, some pastoral counselors might form their own "rule" to make the choice regarding the best direction for counseling to take. One rule might be,

"Take the biggest problem first." Another might be, "Take on the eas-iest presenting problem first." In our view, neither of these honors the counselee as the one who knows what is best. In Joan's case, the coun-selor approached this dilemma with a simple question: "Which of these problems do you feel capable of facing right now?" With this question, the pastoral counseling process began with Joan choosing the direction of each session, and the counselor held firmly to Joan's wisdom and immediate capacity for change.

Finally, some pastoral counselors follow their own competency-based counseling agenda rather than hearing the counselees' stories. Some research (Kuehl 1987) has found that counselees plan their sto-ries and agenda before coming to the counseling session, often to the point of choreographing storytelling to weave a particular view. We have found that counselees have their own ideas about what is *supposed* to happen in counseling, and moving too far afield of these ideas often creates an adversarial relationship. Rather than cutting off counselee stories to stay with the "map," we suggest one guide counselee stories to their conclusions so that the stories can be told efficiently. You might guide stories in several ways. First, when a counselee story has gone on for some time, we simply ask, "Can you tell me how much time you will need to tell me enough of your story so we can begin?" Also, we have used the following question to encourage succinct storytelling: "How will I know that I have enough of your story to begin counsel-ing with you?" Finally, a useful question that evolves from Milton Erickson's "illusion of choice" intervention is this: "How much longer do you believe you will need to relate your story—ten minutes or fif-teen minutes?" If we find ourselves working toward goal-setting and the counselee interrupts with phrases such as, "Oh—you have to understand something" or "I forgot to tell you . . ." then we simply allow the counselee to relate that particular point before asking permis-sion to continue. We have found that counselees will tell us their stories until they are *complete enough*, not until they are completely told. If we interrupt and do not allow enough of the story to be told, then coun-selees will simply interrupt us later to fill in the "blanks" they believe we must have to be effective.

Finally, some pastoral counselors become "solution-forced" when they embrace only the methods without adopting the assumptions and foundational ideas of competency-based counseling. Interventions such as the miracle question and solution-oriented goal setting are tempting because of their supposed simplicity; however, merely because a model seems simple does not mean it is easy to implement. Becoming a consistent competency-based pastoral counselor requires disciplined curiosity, continuous development of respect for counselee resourcefulness, and careful cultivation of one's expertise as a counseling pastor. May God grant you the grace to sustain you in this adventure!

NOTES

Introduction

1. In every counseling example, the names and identifiable specifics have been changed in order to maintain confidentiality.

2. See Cockburn, Thomas, and Cockburn 1997; Gale 1992; Gale 1993; Mabery 1993; Metcalf and Thomas 1994; Metcalf et al. 1996; Swint 1994; Thomas 1994b; Quinn 1998.

3. Our colleague and friend Michael Durrant, a psychologist in Sydney, Australia, says that he has one diagnostic category—stuck. He finds this to be the most useful because it fits everyone who comes to see him.

1. Why "Competency-Based" Counseling?

1. A special note of acknowledgment to George Pate, who provided some of the biblical connections.

2. See Cade (1986).

3. I (FNT) first heard this phrase from my friend Dr. Wendel Ray, the premier archivist of the MRI, January, 1995.

2. Assuming a Competency-Based Stance

1. It is interesting to us that the phrase "stages of grief" has moved from description of what people commonly go through to a prescription of correct grieving (what one *must* go through). See Butler and Powers 1996, Durrant and Kowalski 1993, Thomas 1995a.

3. A Map for Competency-Based Counseling, Part I: Getting Oriented

1. This list is adapted from a list of assumptions compiled by Frank Thomas and Michael Durrant and is used with permission.

2. This map is adapted from Durrant & Kowalski (1993) and created with the knowledge and permission of the first author.

3. For a thorough examination of emotions in brief therapy, see Cade and O'Hanlon (1993).

6. Resource Focus: It's Not Just for Counseling Anymore!

1. We prefer to use the word "interview" as opposed to "counseling." A competency approach to premarital work never assumes *a priori* that every couple is in need of counseling.

2. Thanks to the "Communication in Marriage and the Family" classes, 1991–94, at Texas Woman's University for contributing wonderful ideas to this section. A special thanks to Michael Durrant and Linda Metcalf for refining them with me (FNT) in workshop format (Thomas, Metcalf, and Durrant 1993).

REFERENCES

Anderson, H., and H. Goolishian. 1992. The client is the expert: A not-knowing approach to therapy. In *Therapy as social construction,* ed. S. McNamee and K. J. Gergen, 25–39. Newbury Park, Calif.: Sage.

Barnard, C. P., and B. P. Kuehl. 1995. Ongoing evaluation: In-session procedures for enhancing the working alliance and therapy effectiveness. *American Journal of Family Therapy* 23:161–72.

Bateson, G. 1972. *Steps to an ecology of mind.* Northvale, N.J.: Jason Aronson.

———. 1979. *Mind and nature: A necessary unity.* New York: Bantam.

Becvar, R. J., D. S. Becvar, and A. E. Bender. 1982. Let us first do no harm. *Journal of Marital and Family Therapy* 8:385–91.

Berg, I. K. 1991. *Family preservation: A brief therapy workbook.* London: BT Press.

———. 1994. *Family based services: A solution-focused approach.* New York: W. W. Norton.

Berg, I. K., and S. D. de Shazer. 1993. Making numbers talk: Language in therapy. In *The new language of change: Constructive collaboration in psychotherapy,* ed. S. Friedman, 5–24. New York: Guilford.

Berg, I. K., and S. D. Miller. 1992. *Working with the problem drinker: A solution-focused approach.* New York: W. W. Norton.

Bergin, A. E., and S. L. Garfield. 1994. Overview, trends, and future issues. In *Handbook of Psychotherapy and Behavior Change,* 821–30, 4th ed., ed. A. E. Bergin and S. L. Garfield. New York: Wiley.

Birdwhistell, R. L. 1974. The language of the body. In *Human communication: Theoretical explanations,* ed. A. Silverstein, 203–20. New York: Wiley.

———. 1977. Some discussion of ethnography, theory and method. In *About Bateson,* ed. J. Brockman, 103–44. New York: Dutton.

Bodin, A. M. 1981. The interactional view: Family therapy approaches of the Mental Research Institute. In *Handbook of family therapy*, ed. A. S. Gurman and D. P. Kniskern. New York: Brunner/Mazel. 1:267–309.

Boscolo, L., G. Cecchin, L. Hoffman, and P. Penn. 1987. *Milan systemic family therapy*. New York: Basic.

Budman, S. 1981. *Forms of brief therapy*. New York: Guilford.

Burlingame, G. M., A. Fuhriman, S. Paul, and B. M. Ogles. 1989. Implementing a time-limited therapy program: Differential effects of training and experience. *Psychotherapy* 26: 303–13.

Butler, W. R., and K. V. Powers. 1996. Solution-focused grief therapy. In *Handbook of solution-focused brief therapy*, ed. S. Miller, M. Hubble, and B. Duncan, 228–47. San Francisco: Jossey-Bass.

Cade, B. 1986. The reality of "reality" (or the "reality" of reality.) *The American Journal of Family Therapy* 14:49–56.

———. 1994. Treating the house like a hotel: From simile to metaphor. *Case Studies in Brief and Family Therapy* 8(1):5–14.

Cade, B., and W. H. O'Hanlon. 1993. *A brief guide to brief therapy*. New York: W. W. Norton.

Casey, A. M. 1993. The process of change in parent-child relationships due to adolescent growth: Family explanations. Thesis, Texas Woman's University.

Cockburn, J. T., F. N. Thomas, and O. J. Cockburn. 1997. Solution-focused therapy and psychosocial adjustment to orthopedic rehabilitation in a work hardening program. *Journal of Occupational Rehabilitation* 7(2):97–105.

Coontz, S. 1992. *The way we never were: American families and the nostalgia trap*. New York: Basic Books.

Currant, D. 1983. *Traits of a healthy family*. New York: Ballantine.

———. 1987. *Stress and the healthy family*. New York: Harper and Row.

D'Andrade, R. 1986. Three scientific world views and the covering law model. In *Metatheory in social science*, ed. D. W. Fiske and R. A. Shweder, 19–41. Chicago: University of Chicago Press.

de Jong, P., and I. K. Berg. 1998. *Interviewing for solutions*. Pacific Grove, Calif.: Brooks/Cole.

de Jong, P., and L. E. Hopwood. 1996. Outcome research on treatment conducted at the Brief Family Therapy Center, 1992-1993. In *Handbook of solution-focused brief therapy*, ed. S. Miller, M. Hubble, and B. Duncan, 272–98. San Francisco: Jossey-Bass.

de Shazer, S. 1975. Brief therapy: Two's company. *Family Process* 14:79–93.

———. 1978. Brief hypnotherapy of two sexual dysfunctions: The crystal ball technique. *American Journal of Clinical Hypnosis* 20: 203–8.

———. 1985. *Keys to solution in brief therapy.* New York: W. W. Norton.

———. 1988. *Clues: Investigating solutions in brief therapy.* New York: W. W. Norton.

———. 1990. What is it about brief therapy that works? In *Brief therapy: Myths, methods, and metaphors,* ed. J. K. Zeig, and S. G. Gilligan. New York: Brunner/Mazel.

———. 1991. *Putting difference to work.* New York: W. W. Norton.

———. 1994. *Words were originally magic.* New York: Norton.

———. 1998. Personal communication on 2, June.

de Shazer, S., I. K. Berg, E. Lipchik, E. Nunnally, A. Molnar, W. Gingerich, and M. Weiner-Davis. 1986. Brief therapy: Focused solution development. *Family Process* 25:207–22.

Durrant, M. 1993. *Residential treatment: A cooperative, competency-based approach to therapy and program design.* New York: W. W. Norton.

———. 1995. *Creative strategies for school problems.* New York: W. W. Norton.

———. 1996. Personal communication in June.

Durrant, M., and K. M. Kowalski. 1990. Overcoming the effects of sexual abuse: Developing a self-perception of competence. In *Ideas for therapy with sexual abuse,* ed. M. Durrant and C. White, 65–110. Adelaide, S. Australia: Dulwich Centre Publications.

———. 1993. Enhancing views of competence. In *The new language of change: Constructive collaboration in psychotherapy,* ed. S. Friedman, 107–37. New York: Guilford.

Efron, D. 1994. Commentary. *Journal of Systemic Therapies* 13:38–41.

Efron, D., and K. Veenendaal. 1993. Suppose a miracle doesn't happen: The non-miracle option. *Journal of Systemic Therapies* 12:11–18.

Fisch, R. 1994. Basic elements in the brief therapies. In *Constructive therapies,* ed. M. F. Hoyt, 126–39. New York: Guilford.

Fisher, S. 1980. The use of time limits in brief psychotherapy: A comparison of six-session, twelve-session, and unlimited treatment with families. *Family Process* 19:377–92.

———. 1984. Time-limited brief therapy with families: A one-year follow-up study. *Family Process* 23:101–6.

Friedman, S. 1993. Does the "miracle question" always create miracles? *Journal of Systemic Therapies* 12:71–4.

Furman, B., and T. Ahola. 1992a. *Pickpockets on a nudist camp: The systemic revolution in psychotherapy.* Adelaide, S. Australia: Dulwich Centre Publications.

———. 1992b. *Solution talk: Hosting therapeutic conversations.* New York: W. W. Norton.

Gale, J. 1992. When research interviews are more therapeutic than therapy interviews. *The Qualitative Report.* http://www.nova.edu/ssss/QR/QR1-4/gale.html.

———. 1993. A field guide to qualitative inquiry and its clinical relevance. *Contemporary Family Therapy: An International Journal* 15:73–91.

Garfield, S. L. 1978. Research on client variables in psychotherapy. In *Handbook of psychotherapy and behavior change,* 2d ed., ed. S. L. Garfield and A. E. Bergin. New York: Wiley.

———. 1981. Psychotherapy: A forty-year appraisal. *American Psychologist* 2:174–83.

———. 1994. Research on client variables in psychotherapy. In *Handbook of psychotherapy and behavior change,* 4th ed., ed. S. L. Garfield and A. E. Bergin, 190–228. New York: Wiley.

George, C. F., with W. Bird. 1994. *The coming church revolution: Empowering leaders for the future.* Grand Rapids, Mich.: Fleming H. Revell.

George, E., C. Iveson, and H. Ratner. 1990. *Problem to solution: Brief therapy with individuals and families.* London: BT Press.

Gergen, K. J. 1994. *Realities and relationships: Soundings in social construction.* Cambridge, Mass.: Harvard University Press.

Getzels, J. W. 1982. The problem of the problem. In *Question framing and response consistency,* ed. R. M. Hogarth, 37–49. San Francisco: Jossey-Bass.

Giblin, P. 1994. Premarital preparation: Three approaches. *Pastoral Psychology* 42(3): 147–61.

Glasersfeld, E. von. 1984. An introduction to radical constructivism. In *The invented reality,* ed. P. Watzlawick, 17–40. New York: W. W. Norton.

Guerin, P. J., and E. G. Pendagast. 1976. Family therapy: Theory and practice. New York: Gardner Press.

Gurin, G., J. Veroff, and S. Feld. 1960. *Americans view their mental health: A nationwide interview survey.* New York: Wiley.

Gurin, J. 1990. Remaking our lives. *American Health* (March) 50–52.

Haley, J. 1976. *Problem solving therapy: New strategies for effective family therapy.* San Francisco: Jossey-Bass.

Harré, R., and P. F. Secord. 1972. *The explanation of social behavior.* Oxford: Basil Blackwell.

Heath, A., and L. Tharp. 1991. What therapists say about supervision. Paper presented at the American Association for Marriage and Family Therapy Annual Conference, November, in Dallas, Texas.

Henderson, D., J. Gartner, J. Greer, and B. Estadt. 1992. Who sees a pastoral counselor? An empirical study of client characteristics. *Journal of Pastoral Care* 46(2): 87–94.

Hoffman, L. 1981. *Foundations of family therapy.* New York: Basic.

Keeney, B. P. 1983. *Aesthetics of Change.* New York: Guilford.

————. 1988. The work of Robert Shaw. Unpublished manuscript.

Korzybski, A. 1973. *Science and sanity,* 4th ed. Clinton, Mass.: Colonial Press.

Koss, M. P., and J. N. Butcher. 1986. Research on brief psychotherapy. In *Handbook of psychotherapy and behavior change,* 3d ed., ed. S. L. Garfield and A. E. Bergin, 627–70. New York: Wiley.

Koss, M. P., and J. Shiang. 1994. Research on brief psychotherapy. In *Handbook of psychotherapy and behavior change,* 4th ed., ed. S. L. Garfield and A. E. Bergin, 664–700. New York: Wiley.

Kowalski, K., and R. Kral. 1989. The geometry of solution: Using the scaling technique. *Family Therapy Case Studies* 4(1): 59–66.

Kuehl, B. P. 1987. The voice of the family: An ethnography of family therapy. Ph.D. diss., Texas Tech University.

————. 1995. The solution-oriented genogram. Paper presented at the AAMFT Annual Conference, October, in Chicago, Illinois.

Kuehl, B. P., and C. Barnard. 1993. Utilizing client-generated instructional feedback. Paper presented at the AAMFT Annual Conference, in Anaheim, California.

Kulka, R., J. Veroff, and E. Douvan. 1979. Social class and the use of professional help for personal problems. *Journal of Health and Social Behavior* 20:2–17.

Lambert, M. J., D. A. Shapiro, and A. E. Bergin. 1986. The effectiveness of psychotherapy. In *Handbook of psychotherapy and behavior change,* 3d ed., ed. S. L. Garfield and A. E. Bergin, 157–211. New York: Wiley.

Lankton, S. R. 1990. Just do good therapy. In *Brief therapy: myths, methods, and metaphors,* ed. J. K. Zeig and S. G. Gilligan, 62–77. New York: Brunner/Mazel.

Lankton, S. R., C. H. Lankton, and W. J. Matthews. 1991. Eriksonian family therapy. In *Handbook of family therapy,* ed. A. S. Gurman and D. P. Kniskern. New York: Brunner/Mazel. 2:239–83.

Larson, D., A. Hohmann, L. Kessler, K. Meador, J. Boyd, and E. McSherry. 1988. The couch and the cloth: The need for linkage? *Hospital and Community Psychiatry* 39:1064–69.

Lau, G., and R. Steele. 1990. An empirical study of the pastoral mental health involvement model. *Journal of Psychology and Theology* 18(3):261–69.

Lazarus, A. A., and A. Fay. 1990. Brief psychotherapy: Tautology or oxymoron? In *Brief Therapy: Myths, methods, and metaphors,* ed. J. K. Zeig and S. G. Gilligan, 36–51. New York: Brunner/Mazel.

Lester, A. D. 1995. *Hope in pastoral care and counseling.* Louisville, Ky.: Westminster John Knox Press.

Lipchick, E. 1988. Interviewing with a constructive ear. *Dulwich Centre Newsletter* Winter: 3–7.

———.1993. "Both/and" solutions. In *The new language of change: Constructive collaboration in psychotherapy,* ed. S. Friedman, 25–49. New York: Guilford.

Lowe, D. 1986. Counseling activities and referral practices of ministers. *Journal of Psychology and Christianity* 5(1):22–29.

Lyman, B. J., C. L. Storm, and C. D. York. 1995. Rethinking assumptions about trainees' life experience. *Journal of Marital and Family Therapy* 21:193–203.

Mabery, L. 1993. An ethnography of family change: The experience of strategic therapy. Ph.D. diss., Texas Woman's University.

Martin, J., A. Casey, L. Chenowith, and F. Thomas. 1996. The process of change in parent-child relationships due to adolescent growth: Family explanations. *Texas Association of Family and Consumer Sciences Research Journal* (May) 1(1):12–13.

Maxwell, J. C. 1995. *Developing the leaders around you.* Nashville: Thomas Nelson Publishers.

McCann, R. 1962. *The churches and mental health.* New York: Basic.

McGoldrick, M., and R. Gerson. 1985. *Genograms in family assessment.* New York: W. W. Norton.

McKeel, A. J. 1996. A clinician's guide to research on solution-focused brief therapy. In *Handbook of solution-focused brief therapy,* ed. S. Miller, M. Hubble, and B. Duncan, 251–71. San Francisco: Jossey-Bass.

Metcalf, L. 1993. *The pragmatics of change in solution focused brief family therapy: Ethnographic interviews with couples and their therapists.* Ph.D. diss., Texas Woman's University.

Metcalf, L., and F. N. Thomas. 1994. Client and therapist perceptions of solution-focused brief therapy: A qualitative analysis. *Journal of Family Psychotherapy* 5:49–66.

Metcalf, L., F. N. Thomas, S. D. Miller, M. A. Hubble, and B. Duncan. 1996. What works in solution-focused brief therapy: A qualitative analysis of client and therapist perceptions. In *Handbook of solution-focused brief therapy,* ed. S. Miller, M. Hubble, and B. Duncan, 335–49. San Francisco: Jossey-Bass.

Miller, S., M. A. Hubble, and B. Duncan. 1995. No more bells and whistles. *Networker* 53–63.

———. 1996. *Handbook of solution-focused brief therapy: Foundations, applications, and research.* San Francisco: Jossey-Bass.

———. 1997. *Escape from Babel: Toward a unifying language for psychotherapy practice.* New York: W. W. Norton.

Nardone, G., and P. Watzlawick. 1993. *The art of change.* San Francisco: Jossey-Bass.

National Institute of Mental Health. 1979. *Report of the work group on health insurance, November 1974.* Cited in J. A. Ciarlo, Annual evaluation report for 1975 of the Northwest Denver Mental Health Center. In *Reporting program evaluations: Two sample community mental health center annual reports,* ed. C. Windle. Rockville, Md.: U.S. Department of Health, Education, and Welfare.

Newfield, N. A., B. P. Kuehl, H. P. Joanning, and W. H. Quinn. 1990. A mini-ethnography of the family therapy of adolescent drug abuse: The ambiguous experience. *Alcoholism Treatment Quarterly* 7:57–79.

Nylund, D., and V. Corsiglia. 1994. Becoming solution-focused forced in brief therapy: Remembering something important we already knew. *Journal of Systemic Therapies* 13:5-12.

O'Hanlon, W. H. 1992. Personal communication in January.

O'Hanlon, W. H. and S. Beadle. 1994. A field guide to PossibilityLand: Possibility therapy methods. Omaha, Nebr.: The Center Press.

O'Hanlon, W. H., and P. Hudson. 1995. *Stop blaming, start loving! A solution-oriented approach to improving your relationship.* New York: W. W. Norton.

O'Hanlon, W. H., and M. Weiner-Davis. 1989. *In search of solutions.* New York: W. W. Norton.

O'Hanlon, W. H., and J. Wilk. 1987. *Shifting contexts: The generation of effective psychotherapy.* New York: Guilford.

Olson, D., D. Fornier, and J. Druckman. 1992. *Prepare/Enrich.* Minneapolis: Life Innovations.

Palazzoli, M. S., L. Boscolo, G. Cecchin, and G. Prata. 1978. *Paradox and counterparadox.* London: Jason Aronson.

Pekarik, G., and M. Wierzbicki. 1986. The relationship between clients' expected and actual treatment duration. *Psychotherapy* 23:532–34.

Quinn, W. H. 1998. The client speaks out: Three domains of meaning. *Journal of Family Psychotherapy* 7:71–93.

Rabkin, R. 1986. What is mental health? In *Evolving models for family change,* ed. H. C. Fishman and B. L. Rosman, 214–26. New York: Guilford.

Ray, W. A., and J. H. Weakland, eds. 1995. *Propagations: Thirty years of influence from the Mental Research Institute.* New York: Haworth Press.

Rogers, M. 1985. Needs assessment in the development of a clergy consultation service: A key informant approach. *Journal of Psychology and Theology* 13:50–60.

Segal, L. 1991. Brief therapy: The MRI approach. In *Handbook of family therapy,* 2:71–99, ed. A. S. Gurman and D. P. Knickern. New York: Brunner/Mazel.

Simon, D. 1994. Suppose a miracle doesn't happen: The non-miracle option. *Journal of Systemic Therapies* 13:16–17.

Simon, F. B., H. Stierlin, and L. C. Wynne. 1985. *The language of family therapy: A systemic vocabulary and sourcebook.* New York: Family Process Press.

Smith, M. L., G. V. Glass, and T. I. Miller. 1980. *The benefits of psychotherapy.* Baltimore: Johns Hopkins University Press.

Stinnet, N. 1980. *Family Strengths: Positive models for family life.* Proceedings of 2d of a series of meetings at University of Nebraska, Lincoln, in 1979. Lincoln: University of Nebraska Press.

———. 1981. *Family Strengths 3: Roots of well-being.* Proceedings of 3d of a series of meetings at University of Nebraska, Lincoln, in 1980. Lincoln: University of Nebraska Press.

Stone, H. W. 1994. *Brief pastoral counseling.* Minneapolis, Minn.: Fortress Press.

Swann, W. B., Jr., T. Giuliano, and D. M. Wegner. 1982. Where leading questions can lead: The power of conjecture in social interaction. *Journal of Personality and Social Psychology* 42:1025–35.

Swint, J. 1994. Clients' experiences of therapeutic change: A qualitative study. Ph.D. diss., Texas Woman's University.

Talmon, M. 1990. *Single-session therapy.* San Francisco: Jossey-Bass.

Taube, C. A., B. J. Burnes, and L. G. Keesler. 1984. Patients of psychiatrists and psychologists in office-based practice: 1980. *American Psychologist* 39:1435–47.

Thomas, F. N. 1994a. Solution-oriented supervision: The coaxing of expertise. *Family Journal: Counseling and Therapy for Couples and Families,* 2(1):11–18.

———. 1994b. The experience of solution-oriented therapy: Post-therapy client interviewing. *Case Studies in Brief Family Therapy* 8:47–58.

———. 1995a. The further you travel, the more your views change. *Koinonia Annual* 2:33–50.

———. 1995b. Genograms and competence: Fashioning meaning through alternative application. *News of the Difference* 4(1):9–11.

———. 1996. Solution-focused supervision: The coaxing of expertise. In *Handbook of solution-focused brief therapy,* ed. S. Miller, M. Hubble, and B. Duncan, 128–51. San Francisco: Jossey-Bass.

Thomas, F. N., L. Metcalf, and M. Durrant. 1993. *"What do you do well?" Solution-oriented wellness.* A workshop presented by F. N. Thomas, L. Metcalf, and M. Durrant at the Annual Conference of the American Association for Marriage and Family Therapy, in Anaheim, California, on 9 October.

Todd, T. A., H. Joanning, L. Enders, L. Mutchler, and F. N. Thomas. 1990. Using ethnographic interviews to create a more cooperative client-therapist relationship. *Journal of Family Psychotherapy* 1(3):51–63.

Tomm, K. 1991. Tell me Carl, where do I exist? In *Strange encounters with Carl Auer,* ed. G. Weber and F. B. Simon, 29–40. New York: W. W. Norton.

Veroff, J., R. Kulka, and E. Dorran. 1981. *Mental Health in America.* New York: Wiley.

Virkler, H. 1979. Counseling demands, procedures, and preparation of parish ministers: A descriptive study. *Journal of Psychology and Theology* 7:271–80.

Walter, J., and J. Peller. 1992. *Becoming solution-focused in brief therapy.* New York: Brunner/Mazel.

Watzlawick, P. 1990. Therapy is what you say it is. In *Brief therapy: Myths, methods, and metaphors,* ed. J. K. Zeig and S. G. Gilligan, 55–61. New York: Brunner/Mazel.

Watzlawick, P., J. H. Weakland, and R. Fisch. 1974. *Change: Principles of problem formation and problem resolution.* New York: W. W. Norton.

Weakland, J. H. 1990. Myths about brief therapy: myths of brief therapy. In *Brief Therapy: Myths, methods, and metaphors,* ed. J. K. Zeig and S. G. Gilligan, 100–110. New York: Brunner/Mazel.

Weakland, J. H., R. Fisch, P. Watzlawick, and A. M. Bodin. 1974. Brief therapy: Focused problem resolution. *Family Process* 13:141–68.

Weiner-Davis, M. 1992. *Divorce busting: A revolutionary and rapid program for staying together.* New York: Summit.

———. 1995. *Fire your shrink!* New York: Summit.

Weiner-Davis, M., S. de Shazer, and W. Gingerich. 1987. Building on pretreatment change to construct the therapeutic solution: An exploratory study. *Journal of Marital and Family Therapy* 13(4):359–63.

Welch, R. 1973. *We really do need each other.* Nashville: Impact Books.

Whitaker, C. 1989. *Midnight musings of a family therapist.* New York: W. W. Norton.

———. 1990. Personal communication in February.

White, M. 1989. The externalization of the problem and the re-authoring of lives and relationships. In *Selected Papers,* 5–28. Adelaide, South Australia: Dulwich Centre Publications.

———. 1991. Deconstruction and therapy. *Dulwich Centre Newsletter* 3:21–40.

White, M, and D. Epston. 1990. *Narrative means to therapeutic ends.* New York: W. W. Norton.

Wilson, G. L., J. Keyton, G. D. Johnson, C. Geiger, and J. C. Clark. 1993. Church growth through member identification and commitment: A congregational case study. *Review of Religious Research* 34(3):259–72.

Zeig, J. K., and S. G. Gilligan, eds. 1990. *Brief therapy: Myths, methods, and metaphors.* New York: Brunner/Mazel.